Dr. Bruce H. Wilkinson

A BIBLICAL
PORTRAIT
OF
MARRIAGE

COURSE WORKBOOK

A BIBLICAL PORTRAIT OF MARRIAGE

Executive Editor: Dr. Bruce H. Wilkinson
Project Director: Gary G. Fallon
Editors: William M. Kruidenier
Mary Lee Griffith
Art Director: Randy Drake
Production: Lois Gable

© 2001, 2008 by Walk Thru the Bible.
All rights reserved.

Printed in the USA.

A Biblical Portrait of Marriage and related products are published by Walk Thru the Bible ®.

Publishing and product inquiries:
4201 North Peachtree Rd.
Atlanta, GA 30341-1362 USA
1-800-763-5433
www.walkthru.org

No part of *A Biblical Portrait of Marriage*, whether audio, video, or print, may be reproduced in any form without written permission from Walk Thru the Bible.

The Scripture quotations in this publication are from the New King James Version. Copyright © 1979, 1980, 1982, 1990 Thomas Nelson, Inc.

For more than three decades, Walk Thru the Bible has created discipleship materials and cultivated leadership networks that together are reaching millions of people globally through live events, print publications, audiovisual curricula, radio, television, and the Internet. Known for innovative methods and high-quality resources, we serve the whole body of Christ across denominational, cultural, and national lines. Through our strong and cooperative international partnerships, we are strategically positioned to address the church's greatest need: developing mature, committed, and spiritually reproducing believers.

Walk Thru the Bible communicates the truths of God's Word in a way that makes the Bible readily accessible to anyone. We are committed to developing user-friendly resources that are Bible-centered, of excellent quality, lifechanging for individuals, and catalytic for churches, ministries, and movements; and we are committed to maintaining our global reach through strategic partnerships while adhering to the highest levels of integrity in all we do.

Walk Thru the Bible partners with the local church worldwide to fulfill its mission, helping people "walk thru" the Bible with greater clarity and understanding. Live events and small group curricula are taught in over 50 languages by more than 60,000 people in nearly 60 countries, and more than 100 million devotionals have been packaged into daily magazines, books, and other publications that reach over five million people each year. And, in addition to our ever-expanding stock of newly created curricula, we have recently updated Walk Thru the Bible "classics" from every era of our history into digital formats. These resources, new and old, continue to bear fruit in churches, ministries, and individual lives throughout the world.

Walk Thru the Bible

A BIBLICAL PORTRAIT OF MARRIAGE

Dr. Bruce H. Wilkinson

SESSION	TITLE	PAGE
	Introduction	i–vi
1	Leaving	1.1
2	Cleaving	2.1
3	Helper	3.1
4	Submitting	4.1
5	Leader	5.1
6	Loving	6.1
7	In–Laws	7.1
8	Money	8.1
9	Sex	9.1
10	Romance	10.1
11	Communication	11.1
12	Loyalty	12.1
	Marriage Resources	vii-xii

CONTENTS

How It All Works.

A GUIDE FOR MAKING YOUR SEMINAR PROFITABLE!

A Class Notes

Course Workbooks have ample room for taking notes throughout this series. Key points and Scripture verses appear on the video screen during each session to ensure accurate recording by course participants.

B Evaluations, Interaction, and Projects

After listening to Dr. Wilkinson, participants take a self-evaluation "quiz" to assess their own marriage relationship. Group interaction questions plus a project round out this session.

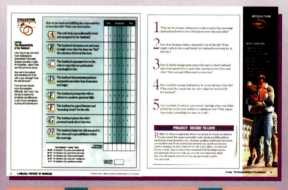

C Bible Studies

For further insight, five Bible studies are available in the Workbook for each session. Participants are encouraged to "dig deeper" using these Scriptures as the basis for additional study.

D Devotionals

Daily devotional guides are provided to personalize the course and discover points of application. Participants read real-life scenarios and consider how the truth of Scripture can impact their own marriage.

iv A BIBLICAL PORTRAIT OF MARRIAGE

© 1995 by Dr. Bruce H. Wilkinson and Walk Thru the Bible Ministries, Inc. Do not reproduce.

Meet the Ethridges!

FROM DRAMAS TO DEVOTIONALS, YOU'LL LOVE THE ETHRIDGES!

Bob Ethridge, Sr.

The family patriarch. Wise, witty, and wonderfully committed to God's best in his marriage—and his children's.

Alice Ethridge

Stable, faithful, and loving helper to Bob, Alice's heart and home are full of love and Godly counsel for her family.

Betty

Oldest daughter of Bob and Alice. A widow who manages well despite losing the love of her life. Sweet and practical.

Bob, Jr.

Bob's and Alice's middle child. Laid back, good guy, very close to his dad. Supervisor at a local plant.

Deb

Bob's wife. She tackles life and love head-on through good times and bad. Sensitive yet strong, loyal to her husband.

Lillith

Youngest child of Bob and Alice, she is a hard-driving bank vice-president, now divorced. Dominant, independent, bitter.

Dwayne

A college junior, Dwayne is Betty's only child. Engaged to be married, has a positive perspective on life and the future.

Bobby

Teenage son of Bob and Deb. Cocky, rowdy, typical teen, growing up too fast for his parents, but too slow for himself!

Kim

Kim is Bobby's Jr. High age sister. Emotional, trendy, full of questions and contradictions. A typical adolescent.

Allison

Lillith's only child. Pre-school, outgoing, full of energy. Caught in the struggle between her mother and dad.

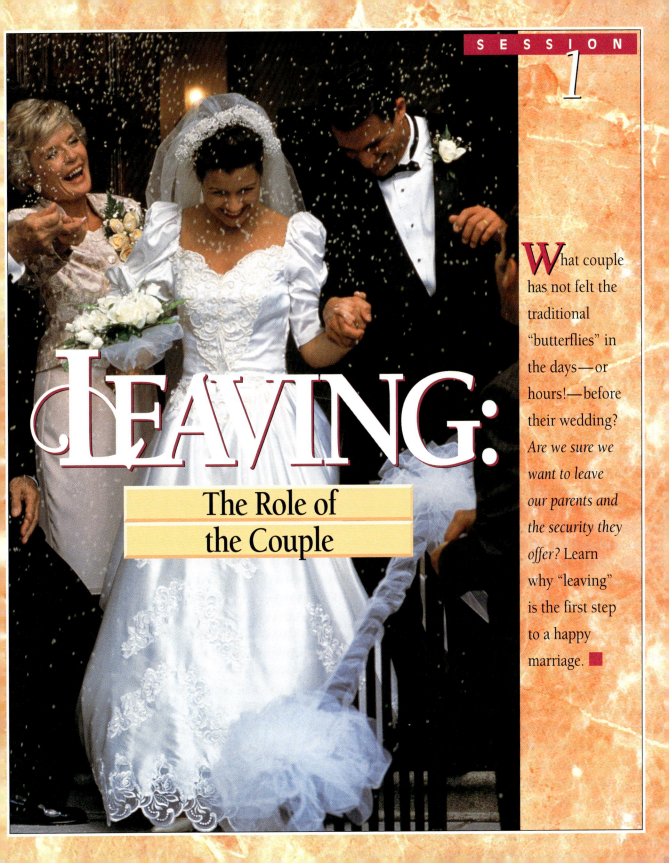

SESSION 1

Leaving:
The Role of the Couple

What couple has not felt the traditional "butterflies" in the days—or hours!—before their wedding? *Are we sure we want to leave our parents and the security they offer?* Learn why "leaving" is the first step to a happy marriage.

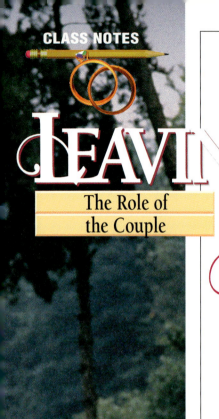

LEAVING: The Role of the Couple

INTRODUCTION

 hat are the secrets to a happy marriage (Genesis 2:24)?

1. Therefore a man shall _____ his father and mother,

2. And _____ to his wife,

3. And they shall become _____ _____.

 hat are the basic reasons why people don't leave?

1. _____ problem

2. _____ problem

How is the word "leave" defined in the Hebrew language (the language in which the Old Testament was written)?

1. To _____
2. To _____
3. To _____

_____
_____

In what ways should the husband and wife leave?

1. Leave _____.
2. Leave _____.
3. Leave _____.

_____
_____

CONCLUSION

_____
_____
_____

EVALUATION

Leaving: The Role of the Couple

This evaluation is designed to help both spouses assess how well they have fulfilled the instruction to *leave* as presented in this session. Try to rate each statement in light of what is generally true at this time in your marriage.

Answer from the perspective of how you as a couple have succeeded at leaving, rather than answering just from your individual point of view. Should your scores be dissimilar, use this as an opportunity to explore why your perceptions differ. This could be an excellent time to reaffirm the steps you need to take to complete the leaving process more fully in your marriage.

Couples, evaluate how fully you have experienced the leaving process. Total your score below.

		False			Sometimes			True
A	We were successful in leaving our parents when we got married.	1	2	3	4	5	6	7
B	Leaving family and other close relationships has been a harmonious process for us.	1	2	3	4	5	6	7
C	Even though we may have problems from time to time in our marriage, we resist the temptation to run home to our parents.	1	2	3	4	5	6	7
D	Both of us are free from manipulation or control by our parents.	1	2	3	4	5	6	7
E	Neither of us has tried to force our spouse to be like one of our own parents.	1	2	3	4	5	6	7
F	We have established our own residence away from our parents' home.	1	2	3	4	5	6	7
G	We are not financially dependent upon either set of parents.	1	2	3	4	5	6	7
H	While we may enjoy frequent talks or visits with our parents, our sense of emotional well-being does not depend on such communication.	1	2	3	4	5	6	7

The Couple's "Leaving" Score

- **48–56** We love our home.
- **38–47** There's no place like home.
- **28–37** Their house—our home away from home.
- **18–27** Our home, their home—what's the big deal?
- **8–17** Their house *is* our home.

Column Subtotals:

GRAND TOTAL:

1 Which do you think is the greatest problem in most marriages—leaving or cleaving? Why?

2 How do some parents make it very difficult for their children to leave? What kinds of statements and actions are used by parents to "manipulate" a young couple to keep them from leaving completely?

3 How would you describe men or women who are still too strongly attached to their parents? How does a husband or wife feel if the spouse's loyalty is divided?

4 What kinds of activities or communication can be appropriate between a new couple and their parents? When can such activities be detrimental to the leaving process?

5 What could parents do that would enable the new couple to leave with joy and freedom? What steps could a new couple take to ensure that leaving is complete?

PROJECT: DECIDE TO LEAVE

Do either (or both) of you still evidence a failure to leave your parents completely? Are there any other relationships or activities which you find hold a higher priority in your life than your spouse? **Discuss** the one or two situations that bring the greatest conflict in your marriage that are rooted in a failure to leave. **Strategize** how you will each deal with the most difficult situation. **Role play** how and what you will respectfully say to your parents when certain opportunities arise to demonstrate your commitment to make your marriage a higher priority than your relationship with anyone or anything else.

INTERACTION

On the Lighter Side

"Sign on the door to a marriage license office: 'Out to lunch—think it over!'"

"Most girls seem to marry men like their fathers. Maybe that's the reason so many mothers cry at weddings."

"A mother may hope that her daughter will get a better husband than she did, but she knows her son will never get as good a wife as his father did."

BIBLE STUDY

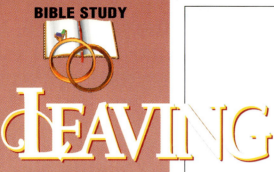

LEAVING

So Long, See You Later, Good-bye

What picture comes to your mind when you think of saying, "Good-bye"? Your mom standing on the sidewalk dabbing at her eyes? Your dad giving you a bear hug right before you leave? A married daughter waving out the window as she drives down the street? A married man strangely quiet and subdued during the drive "home" from visiting his parents?

Although some "good-bye's" can be very joyful, they are usually quite emotional. And they are particularly emotional when it comes to parents letting go of their sons or daughters.

God's Word presents clear direction concerning leaving. These Bible study questions are designed to encourage you to consider how Biblical principles can have personal application to you in your marriage.

1 Leaving's Design
Mark 10:6–8

Since when has "leaving" been part of God's design for marriage?

Why does a newly married couple need to leave their parents?

What did "leaving" involve in your marriage?

If you had to leave all over again, what would you do differently?

2 Leaving's Difficulty
Genesis 2:24

Who is the man (and by implication the woman) instructed to leave?

Why is it so hard for some men and women to leave their parents?

Describe a situation in your marriage in which the husband's difficulty in leaving was demonstrated.

Describe a situation in which it was hard for the wife to leave her parents.

1.6   A BIBLICAL PORTRAIT OF MARRIAGE   © 1995 by Dr. Bruce H. Wilkinson and Walk Thru the Bible Ministries, Inc. Do not reproduce.

3. Leaving's Emotion
Genesis 44:18–22

How did Judah, Joseph's brother, say their father would react if his youngest son were taken away from him?

Why is it so hard for parents to let go of their children?

What attitudes and emotions did your parents express during your "leaving" period (engagement, wedding, and early marriage)?

What were some ways that your parents struggled with letting go when you got married?

What do you wish your parents had done that would have made it easier for you to leave?

4. Complete Leaving
Genesis 39:7–18

What did Joseph leave behind in this passage?

What people or activities must first be left behind in order to properly cleave to one's spouse?

How challenging was it for you to put other friendships or activities in a secondary place to your new spouse?

What kinds of actions did you have to take in order to fulfill the "leaving" command in relationship to those other friendships or activities?

Is there anything (or anyone) in the present that you need to leave so that you can more freely work at your relationship with your spouse?

5. A Good-bye Kiss
Genesis 31:55

How did Laban part from his sons and daughters when Jacob was preparing to take them back to his homeland?

Why is it important that parents let their children go?

As you think ahead toward the time when your own children will leave to get married, what will you do to help them leave?

Will you continue to solidify the leaving process in your own marriage? And will you uphold this principle in relation to your children? Signify your heartfelt intent by initialing and dating this page.

Your initials and date

DEVOTIONAL 1

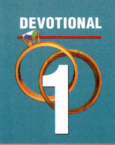

Looking to a New Father

SCRIPTURE
Genesis 2:24a

Therefore a man shall leave his father and mother.

"You won't?" Bob asked his dad. "I don't think so, Son," Bob, Sr., replied. "I suspected you were coming over to talk about your truck, and I've given it a good bit of thought—and prayer, too."

"Well, could you tell me why? You've loaned me money a couple of times in the past. This doesn't seem any different. And I can't afford to replace my truck right now. I'm stuck without this engine overhaul."

"You're right, Bob, I have helped you and Deb in the past. But I'm not sure it was the wisest thing to do. Some men and I were talking at church the other day about how easy it is for our married kids who live close by to still rely on us—for money, for instance—and how our being available actually is a disservice in terms of our children learning to be resourceful and to trust God.

"Scripture says that when you married Deb, you *left* your mother and me—as it should be. And Son, I think part of God's reasoning for that 'leaving' being so clear in Scripture is because it forces you to become stronger, more mature, more dependent on your heavenly Father. What if your mother and I were gone, and your truck engine blew up. How would you handle it then?"

After a moment of silence, Bob reasoned, "I don't know. I guess I'd have to think of something."

"Well, if my being here is keeping you from 'thinking of something,' then let's play like I'm not here and start thinking and praying about the truck. You're better off in His hands than mine!"

From the Word

What do you think? Was Bob, Sr., being too hard on his son? Or was his counsel good, but a little late?

Scripture would suggest the latter. A common mistake for parents is not to take seriously the words of Genesis 2:24. Parents should insist that those children (especially those sons) who have left home to start their own marriages transfer their material and practical dependence from parents to God. Training for such a transfer should begin prior to marriage, of course, so that the transition is not too abrupt. But, be the transition abrupt or gradual, tardy or on time, it still needs to be made. It's part of becoming a married adult!

For the Heart

Has there been too much of a casual dependence upon either set of parents for things that are actually your responsibility to solve?

Have your parents been unable to move from "parent" to "counselor" because you have failed to sever the financial or emotional umbilical cord? Talk with your spouse about this. Identify the areas where either of you have not yet "left home." Even talk to your parents if necessary to ensure their cooperation.

The next time you are tempted to phone home, call your heavenly Father instead!

A gentle, but firm, push has taught many a young bird to fly.

DEVOTIONAL 2

Learning to Leave

SCRIPTURE
Proverbs 3:1–35

My son, do not forget my law, but let your heart keep my commands; for length of days and long life and peace they will add to you.

(verses 1–2)

"Well, did you men have a good time?" Betty asked as Dwayne came into the house. "I know Mother's apple pie and homemade ice cream are worth a trip home from college, but is that all there was to the meeting?"

"Mom! I'm surprised! This was nothing more than the men of the Ethridge family meeting to discuss the affairs of the world. You know, cigars, brandy, a roaring fire—the whole bit."

"Very funny. Why don't I believe you?"

"Okay, okay. Actually, it made me feel kind of good. Granddad and Uncle Bob wanted to talk about my engagement to Sherry. To be honest, I think they're concerned that since my dad isn't around, I may need someone just to talk about marriage with. And it felt good. You know, they asked lots of questions, and said they wanted to spend some more time together between now and the wedding—just to talk about making the transition to marriage and stuff."

"Well, I confess, I had an idea that's what they wanted. And I'm glad they called. I'm glad you have men like Granddad and Uncle Bob to go to for advice. So, what advice did you get?"

"Actually, it was kind of general, but it really made me think. Granddad quoted a lot from the Book of Proverbs about how youth is God's preparation time for becoming an adult. That you have to mentally and practically get ready to "move out" of the security of your youth—and your home—especially when you get married. Kind of a scary thought, actually, Mom."

"Yes it is, Dwayne. It is indeed."

From the Word

A great truth of Scripture has been largely lost in youth-oriented Western cultures: *Youth is not an end in itself, but is a training time, an apprenticeship, for adulthood.* And marriage is often the dividing line which marks the transition. The Book of Proverbs supports this perspective thoroughly in many passages, for example, chapter three. The teaching a father gives to his son is critical to the son's success in leaving youth and entering adulthood. Unfortunately, many adults suffer in their own marriages as a result of not adequately "leaving" the home of their youth. It is God's plan for parents to so train their children that the children live successful adult (and married) lives of their own.

For the Heart

On a large piece of paper, have each spouse draw out a "map," or a history, of his or her life—high points, low points, parental involvement, your marriage, your relationship to your parents, etc. Include everything you can which might have a bearing on how completely you have made the transition from "their home" to "your home." It is amazing what insights come out of "the big picture."

Then, stand back and look. If you see weak points which seem clear in hindsight, purpose to correct them—for your children's sake as well as your own!

There is a time to learn to leave, followed by a time to leave!

DEVOTIONAL 3

A Hard Kind of Obedience

SCRIPTURE
Acts 20:13–38

Then they all wept freely, and fell on Paul's neck and kissed him, sorrowing most of all for the words which he spoke, that they would see his face no more. And they accompanied him to the ship.

(verses 37–38)

"I'm not totally sure I'm ready for this Dad," Betty said with a hint of genuine reluctance in her voice. Her father, Bob, Sr., smiled understandingly.

"It doesn't happen often and, in your case, it hasn't ever happened. I know Will's death was your initiation into the world of suffering and loneliness, Betty. And I'm sure unconsciously that you've allowed Dwayne to sort of replace Will in your life in a lot of ways. Do you think that's true?"

"I'm sure it is, Dad. And now I'm feeling the same way about his leaving to get married as I did when Will died. I'm just not sure I was expecting the waves of loneliness to come pouring in so quickly—and it hasn't even happened yet! What'll I be like when it does?"

"You'll make it, but not without a few tears. Your mother and I shed a few when you and Will got married. You were our first to leave home, remember? And it was *hard*—the hardest thing I had done up to that point in my life. My, I'll never forget turning you over to Will! Fortunately, our pastor at that time had done a good job of getting your mother and me ready. This may sound a bit dramatic, but it's accurate: Parents have to be prepared for the worst—as if you'll never see your child again after the wedding day. That's how clear your willingness to let them go—really, to send them out!—must be. You're dying to a period of life that will never be repeated with that child. And it hurts."

"It may hurt, Dad, but I know you're right. I'm glad I've got time to get ready."

From the Word

Life is definitely a series of closed and open chapters as we move from one phase of life to another. Closing chapters on significant parts of life is an act of courage, wisdom, and obedience. But it is not without sorrow. The Apostle Paul learned this in his own life when he left the leaders of the church at Ephesus, aware that he would never see them again. These men wept on one another on the day of their parting, yet they knew that for one chapter to open, another must close. Wise are the parents who live this truth, and are willing to endure their own personal loss for their children's ultimate gain. Necessary words are often hard words, and for parents, "Good-bye" is both!

For the Heart

Hopefully, when you and your spouse married, someone had a heart-to-heart talk with you about the reality of separation—what it meant to be leaving your home. And hopefully you achieved a measure of "closure" on the chapter of youth.

It's never too late to gain a healthier perspective! Discuss these questions with your spouse: Was I prepared to leave home when we married? Have I completed that separation process today? What was my greatest loss? What was my greatest gain? What evidence do you see in me that I still cling to the past?

Parting is such sweet sorrow. Don't put it off until tomorrow.

DEVOTIONAL 4

Multiple Masters in Marriage

SCRIPTURE: Matthew 6:24

"No one can serve two masters; for either he will hate the one and love the other, or else he will be loyal to the one and despise the other. You cannot serve God and mammon."

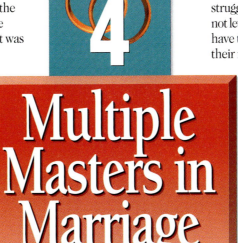

When Bob, Jr., arrived home late that Friday afternoon, the den looked like a garage sale in the making. Deb and her mother were rearranging, sorting, discarding—it was every knickknack for itself!

"Hello, Dorothy! Did you have a safe trip?" Bob asked Deb's mom.

"Hello, Bob! Yes, it was lovely. I got here just in time to help Deb start shaping up the house. Time for spring-cleaning, you know! Deb, I'm going to take this load out to the garbage. I'll be right back."

When they were alone, Deb looked at Bob a bit sheepishly and shrugged her shoulders. "Well, Mom's here. Can you tell?"

"As a matter of fact, I can," Bob replied coolly. "What's going on, Deb?"

"Well, Mom just felt like the house needed an overhaul, and you know how hard it is to tell her 'no.' I decided it was easier to just go ahead and let her have her way than to argue. You're not upset, are you?"

"Not at your mom, Deb. That's the way she is—always will be, I guess. But I am wondering . . . did you remember you and I were supposed to go out to dinner with Tim and Tracey tonight? That's been planned for a couple of weeks, Deb."

"I remembered, Bob. But, I was going to ask you if we could go tomorrow night. Mom is so intent on getting this cleaning and reorganizing done tonight. It seems like it would be pretty thoughtless of me to let her stay here and finish this by herself."

"I see," Bob replied, turning away.

From the Word

What husband or wife has not struggled with a parent who just will not let go? A parent who feels they still have the right to direct the life of their married child? It's common. It's understandable. And it's wrong. Let's see why.

In Scripture, the kingdom of God is presented as a kingdom of choices. For instance, Christ said that no person can serve two masters as top priority. The failure to choose will eventually produce a negative choice. One contender will end up despised and hated while the other is loved! Spouses who do not keep priorities and loyalties clearly in order will offend either a parent or a spouse. And for a spouse, God has already made the decision. Parents are the lower priority.

For the Heart

Can you recall a time when a situation similar to the one described here occurred in your marriage? Or, are your parents reluctant to allow you or your spouse to run your own affairs—be your decisions good or bad? There is perhaps a measure of this tension in every marriage.

Because this situation is predictable and understandable, you can prepare for it. Depending on your situation, and the sensitivity of the parents, action could be anything from a subtle hint to a more forthright conversation. Discuss—and prepare now!—how to maintain loyalties.

If offense is necessary, it is better to offend for what is right.

DEVOTIONAL 5

Please Please Your Wife

**SCRIPTURE
1 Corinthians 7:33**

But he who is married cares about the things of the world—how he may please his wife.

"Mom, this is Bob. I'm afraid I've got some bad news—we need to adjust our plans for this Friday night."

"Oh? Why? Somebody had better be on their deathbed for you all to miss our dinner for Uncle Roy," Alice teased—sort of.

Bob knew his mom was teasing—sort of. This dinner for her brother from the West Coast had been scheduled for a couple of weeks, and had a "be-there-or-else" aura about it already.

"Well, it may be *my* deathbed, Mom, once you and Deb get through with me," Bob laughed to diffuse the tension. "Remember when Deb won the local Garden Club award a few weeks ago for her flowers and landscaping in our yard?"

"Of course," Alice said with distance in her voice.

"Well, the citywide judging's been going on since then, with a big banquet scheduled for Friday night. Deb was fine with missing the banquet to see Uncle Roy, but then they called today to say Deb won second place in the citywide judging. Isn't that great, Mom? And, well, it turns out we need to be at the banquet to see her receive her trophy."

"You mean, 'Deb has to be there,'" Alice said, with the distance growing.

"Technically, yes, but in every other way, it's 'we.' I need to support Deb in this, Mom, and the kids, too. It wouldn't be right for the whole community to be honoring her and her own family not be there. If I have to choose, Mom, which I guess I do, then I have to choose Deb."

From the Word

The words of the Apostle Paul in 1 Corinthians 7:33 have startled many. In light of Christ's teaching to seek first the kingdom of God, it is surprising that Paul would tell a husband that he must focus first on what pleases his wife if he is going to be married. The principle even applies to "the Lord's work"—a wife comes first! If God's work can be "slighted" because of marriage, how much more reasonable is it that a husband's or wife's time with his or her parents might be "slighted" as well? But this is really not a conflict since, in reality, pleasing one's wife is God's command. What a husband does to please his wife is, therefore, "the Lord's work" after all!

For the Heart

Have you or your spouse ever chosen not to use your time or resources to meet your parents' expectations? While married children should make every effort to honor their parents, a thin line exists between honor motivated by respect and compliance motivated by guilt.

Husbands, have you made a firm choice to please your wife above all others—even your parents? Discuss a time when the husband chose to prefer the wife's needs over his parents' desires. How did the parents respond? The wife? How could the process have been improved?

For husbands, pleasing God means first pleasing your wife.

A BIBLICAL PORTRAIT OF MARRIAGE

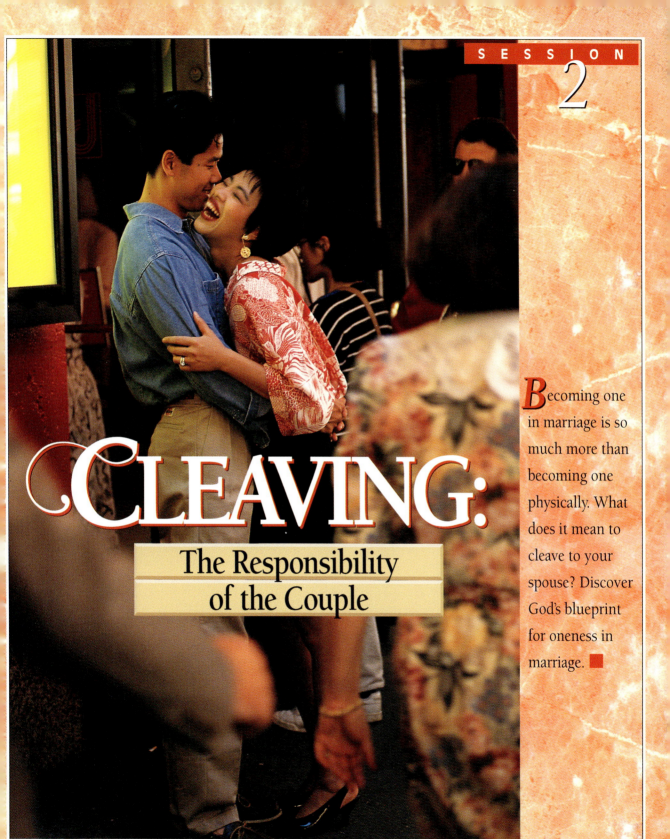

SESSION 2

CLEAVING:
The Responsibility of the Couple

*B*ecoming one in marriage is so much more than becoming one physically. What does it mean to cleave to your spouse? Discover God's blueprint for oneness in marriage. ■

CLASS NOTES

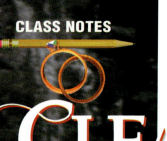

CLEAVING:
The Responsibility of the Couple

INTRODUCTION

_____
_____
_____
_____

What is the key passage on marriage in the Bible?

Therefore a man shall _____ his father and mother and _____ to his wife, and they shall become one flesh (Genesis _____).

_____
_____

How is the word "cleave" defined in the Hebrew language?

1. To _____
2. To be _____ together
3. To _____ _____ together

_____
_____

What must a couple do in order to experience oneness in marriage?

1. Leave everyone else _____.

2. Remain pure _____ (1 Corinthians 7:2–3).

3. Love for the _____ _____.

4. Live at _____ _____ of living.

5. _____ at marital happiness (Deuteronomy 24:5).

6. _____ seventy times seventy.

7. Keep God in the _____ of your marriage.

CONCLUSION

EVALUATION

Cleaving: The Responsibility of the Couple

It is not uncommon to discover that while one spouse has struggled with leaving, the other spouse may find it difficult to cleave. And certain challenges may emerge at different stages in a marriage. In this evaluation, do your best to rate each statement in light of what is generally true at this time in your marriage.

You may discover that how you rate your marriage in this area differs from your spouse's assessment. One of the purposes of using an evaluation is to provide the opportunity for you to discuss your differences and to determine what steps you can take to make your marriage stronger than it is today.

How well do you and your spouse cleave to each other in your marriage? Total your score below.

		False						True
				Sometimes				
A	We are committed to each other for life. Divorce is not an acceptable option.	1	2	3	4	5	6	7
B	Both of us are being careful to avoid the establishment or maintenance of any close opposite-sex friendships.	1	2	3	4	5	6	7
C	We are both committed to reserve the expression of our sexuality only within our marriage.	1	2	3	4	5	6	7
D	We are content with what we have and are not seeking to live at a higher standard than what we can afford.	1	2	3	4	5	6	7
E	We are both making an effort to prevent other people, activities, or responsibilities from infringing on our time for each other.	1	2	3	4	5	6	7
F	Both of us are choosing to forgive hurts before walls are built between us.	1	2	3	4	5	6	7
G	We both guard against vengefully using past hurts to retaliate against our spouse.	1	2	3	4	5	6	7
H	Giving God His rightful place in our marriage is our highest goal as a couple.	1	2	3	4	5	6	7

The Couple's "Cleaving" Score
- **48–56** The Perfect Couple.
- **38–47** A Tight Couple.
- **28–37** Side-by-Side.
- **18–27** A Couple of Individuals.
- **8–17** The Odd Couple.

Column Subtotals:

GRAND TOTAL:

INTERACTION

1 Why is divorce so prevalent in today's society? What would it take to lower the divorce rate?

2 Why do some couples treat their marriage vows so lightly? What do a husband and wife need to believe in order to build a lasting marriage?

3 When either the husband or wife has a close friend of the opposite sex, what complications can that bring into the marriage? How can close friendships of the same sex sometimes bring conflict?

4 Why is it so hard to forgive a spouse? How have you observed a lack of forgiveness being demonstrated within a marriage?

5 Of the couples you have known who appear to be very happily married, how do they work at their marriage relationship?

On the Lighter Side

"A successful marriage is not a gift; it is an achievement."
—Ann Landers

"The divorce rate would be lower if, instead of marrying for better or worse, people would marry for good."

"The man who is forever criticizing his wife's judgment never seems to question her choice of a husband."

PROJECT: LEARN TO CLEAVE

Review the seven principles on how to cleave. **Congratulate** yourselves for the ones that you are both following at this time in your marriage! **Choose** the principle with which you are personally struggling, and **write** it out on a 3x5 card. **Post** that card in a place where you will see it numerous times every day (on the bathroom mirror, above the kitchen sink, on the dashboard of your car, etc.). Every time you look at that card, **pray** and ask the Lord how you could implement that principle within your marriage. You *can* experience greater oneness in your marriage.

BIBLE STUDY

CLEAVING

"Till Death Do Us Part"

It's no cliché—"The most difficult years of marriage are those following the wedding." A good marriage does take a lot of hard work . . . and commitment.

Through these Bible studies, allow God's Word to make an impact on what you believe about marriage as well as what you live in marriage. Obey God's command to cleave to your spouse.

1. Married for Life
Mark 10:9

What perspective did Jesus present of the marriage relationship?

Why is this so hard for many people to accept?

How has your commitment to your spouse affected how you deal with problems in your marriage?

What could you do today for your spouse that would most powerfully affirm your commitment to a lasting marriage?

2. Marital Unity
Matthew 19:6

In the first phrase of this verse, how does Jesus describe the marriage relationship?

What does it mean to be "one" in marriage?

In what aspects of your marriage do you have a oneness of mind and heart?

In what area of your marriage do you and your spouse lack unity or oneness?

What have you experienced as the consequences of a lack of unity?

2.6 A BIBLICAL PORTRAIT OF MARRIAGE

© 1995 by Dr. Bruce H. Wilkinson and Walk Thru the Bible Ministries, Inc. Do not reproduce.

3. Build Your Marriage
Proverbs 14:1

What does the wise woman do?

How would a couple benefit from focusing time, attention, and effort on their own relationship?

In what ways have you sought to build and strengthen your relationship with your spouse?

What could your spouse do that would most clearly demonstrate his or her desire to work at your marriage relationship?

What do you think your spouse would most like you to change as an evidence that you want to develop a stronger marriage?

4. Happily Married
Deuteronomy 24:5

What was the man instructed to do during the first year of marriage?

Why are so many marriages unhappy?

How would you describe a happy marriage?

What are two ways your spouse has brought happiness to you?

What one thing could you do for your mate today that would bring him or her great happiness?

5. Married Under God
Matthew 19:6

Who does Jesus say ultimately "signs" the couple's marriage certificate?

How committed is God to keeping your marriage together?

In what aspect of your marriage do you sense the greatest need for divine intervention to bring healing and restoration?

How committed are you to cooperating with God in the preservation of your marriage?

Will you reaffirm your marriage vows today? Are you committed to doing what is needed to build a lasting love relationship with your spouse? Demonstrate your agreement by initialing and dating this page.

Your initials and date

DEVOTIONAL 1

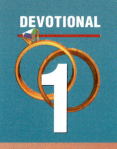

One Plus One Equals One

SCRIPTURE
Genesis 2:24b

And [the man and his wife] shall become one flesh.

"To be perfectly honest, Uncle Bob, it's not easy keeping your mind on your studies. You have to almost wear blinders in order to avoid all the temptation that's around."

Dwayne and his uncle were chatting about college life while Bob finished installing Deb's new washer.

"Yeah, I'll be glad when Sherry and I are married, to end the physical temptation problem. I'm glad God put that part in the Bible about the 'two shall become one flesh'—know what I mean, Uncle Bob?" Dwayne smiled at his uncle.

Bob laid down his wrench and turned to Dwayne. "I do know what you mean, pal. Physical intimacy in marriage is a wonderful thing. And while it does provide the outlet God designed for normal physical desires, you need to know that the verse you're referring to wasn't given by God as an answer to sexual temptation. The verse is really about much more than that."

"Like what?" Dwayne asked.

"Well, like the union between all aspects of two individual lives. Sexually for sure, but in other ways as well. Emotionally, spiritually—every part of both people."

Bob held his hands up in front of him, fingers spread out. "Say this hand is you, and this hand is Sherry. And my fingers are all your individual traits. In marriage, two individuals m·e·r·g·e together," Bob moved his two hands together and clasped them as he spoke, "and become one. Still individuals, but now living as one."

"Hey, I see what you mean!"

From the Word

How well have you and your spouse "merged"? Scripture indicates that marriage is like salvation, having both a positional and an experiential aspect. Positionally, when one believes in Christ, he or she is a Christian at that moment, though learning to live as a Christian is a lifelong task. So it is in marriage. Genesis 2:24 says that a man shall leave his home, be joined to his wife, and *become one flesh*. Once the covenant of marriage is made, husband and wife are one positionally. But learning to perfect and experience their unity takes a lifetime. Regardless of time, oneness is both the reality and the goal in marriage—perfecting that which is possessed.

For the Heart

Apply Bob's "fingers" illustration to your marriage for a moment. Jot down on a piece of paper these five categories: spiritual, physical, financial, personality, and family life. How "merged" are these areas in your lives as a married couple? NOT THAT YOU HAVE TO AGREE ON EACH AREA! But how much more comfortable and unified are you becoming as a couple—as a single functioning unit—in these five areas as your marriage progresses? Jot down a "grade" for each area (5 = together, 1 = not together) and compare notes with your spouse.

Great diversity can be found within the most unified systems.

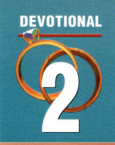

DEVOTIONAL 2

A God-Kind of Promise

SCRIPTURE
Malachi 2:13–15

Yet you say, "For what reason?" Because the Lord has been witness between you and the wife of your youth, with whom you have dealt treacherously; yet she is your companion and your wife by covenant.

(verse 14)

Seven o'clock was coming fast, and Bob and Alice were hurrying to get ready for the church Valentine's Banquet. They were to receive the annual "Covenant Award," given by the pastor and board to the couple in the church most exemplifying the Biblical covenant of marriage—so they wanted to look their best and be on time.

As Alice rifled through the hangers in her closet looking for her favorite dress—bright red, for Valentine's Day—she was growing panicky.

"Bob, you did pick up my dress at the cleaners this afternoon, didn't you?"

Bob froze—toothbrush in mouth—a cold wave of terror washing over him. He had forgotten the red dress.

"Honey, I forgot. I can't believe I did that. But I did—I just plain forgot. I was in such a hurry to get home, thinking I'd be late, that I just . . . I am really sor . . ."

"Oh, Bob, how could you! That's the dress I wanted to wear tonight. Now we're going to have to stand up in front of the whole church with me in some plain old thing! Couldn't you remember one dress?"

"Well, you're right, Alice. I should have remembered. It's my fault, no question. But frankly, I don't think it merits getting upset about, does it?"

"UPSET? Who's UPSET? I just would like to have my dress, that's all!"

"Alice—I said I was sorry! But there's nothing we can do about the dress now, okay? What we *can* do is try to act consistent with the award we're about to receive. Don't you agree?"

From the Word

How easy it is, even in award-winning marriages, to lose sight of the real issue: Biblical love for one another. The kind of love present in marriage is to be so deep, so profound, that it is given the same theological name as the love of Christ for the church. The term "covenant" describes God's love for Israel and His love for the church through Christ. And it also describes marriage. Marriage is first and foremost a covenant. It is an agreement, a pledge, a promise that nothing will be allowed to invalidate the lifelong commitment the covenant partners make to one another. Covenants can withstand all human mistakes—even forgetting to pick up a red dress at the cleaners! (But woe to the husband who forgets!)

For the Heart

Whether you repeated the traditional vows used in most weddings or wrote your own, your vows were the statement of your covenant with each other. The exchanging and wearing of rings publicly announces that covenant.

For richer or poorer, in sickness and in health, says, "I will love you regardless." Have you attacked your covenant partner recently? If so, would you allow your covenant promise to be the motivation to go and apologize? No human error or weakness should be allowed to invalidate your covenant promise.

"It is better not to vow than to vow and not pay." (King Solomon)

DEVOTIONAL 3

Never, Never, Give Up

SCRIPTURE
1 Corinthians 7:10–24

A wife is not to depart from her husband. . . . And a husband is not to divorce his wife.

(verses 10b–11)

"Well, you know Larry was never a very strong Christian, Betty, and so it was probably better that we divorced in the long run. I mean, I know I was no saint during those days either, but I think I was more serious about God than he was."

Lillith and Betty ended up on the subject of Lillith's divorce while spending an evening cooking for Thanksgiving dinner.

"I guess I have to disagree with you somewhat, Lillith. I mean, you could be right, that the divorce put you back in the place you would have been if you hadn't married Larry. Maybe your marriage was unwise in the first place. But I think Scripture talks about not divorcing even if you find yourself married to a non-Christian. You remember—we talked about some of this when you and Larry were considering splitting up."

"I remember, Betty, but I still don't understand it. I didn't understand it then either. I guess that's why we went ahead with it," Lillith sighed.

"Lillith," Betty continued, "maybe the point is that marriage as an institution is more important than either a husband's or wife's enjoyment of it. That could sound like you're supposed to stay married even though you're miserable. But that's not right either. I think God wants us to stay married—but *not* stay miserable. In other words, work to make the marriage better. But whatever you do, don't divorce just because your feelings tell you you've maybe made a mistake and married the wrong person."

"Great. Now I've blown it twice!"

From the Word

Fortunately, for Lillith and for us, it doesn't matter how many times we "blow it" with God. He is always forgiving. But we can avoid needless mistakes by knowing His Word. In this case, the Apostle Paul counsels not to divorce under circumstances like Lillith's. In 1 Corinthians 7:10–24, Paul advises not to leave a spouse, even if he or she is a non-Christian, once you are married. Why? Because apparently a peaceful marriage between a believer and a non-believer is more glorifying to God than divorce. A divorce rips apart something which God allowed to be brought together, and removes God's opportunity to continue His work in the marriage.

For the Heart

Whether there is a divorce in your past or not, the principles of 1 Corinthians 7 are profound and worth considering by all couples.

Consider for a moment the truths discussed here. What evidence is there in your life that God's institution of marriage is honored more than your personal feelings and preferences? Is there a choice that you have made which gives evidence of that fact? Do this: Reaffirm to your spouse as soon as possible your commitment to marriage, and to God's plan that marriage is a permanent institution.

Principles keep us anchored when winds of emotion blow.

DEVOTIONAL 4

What's the Point of Marriage?

SCRIPTURE
Matthew 19:3–9

"So then, they are no longer two but one flesh."

(verse 6a)

Deb sounded hesitant, even cautious, when she interrupted Bob's reading—and he sensed it. Lowering the newspaper, he replied, "What is it, Deb?"

"I need to ask you something. A lady from our neighborhood came by today collecting for the heart fund. I've seen her before, but don't know her, so I invited her in for a minute while I looked for the checkbook. We started talking about families and kids and everything, and I began to notice a pattern in the way she talked—especially anything about money. She said things like 'Jim's lake house,' or 'I pay for the kids' camps,' or 'My money,' or 'His share of the utilities bill.' I don't think I heard her use the word 'we' once in the whole conversation! It sounded like she and her husband were two individuals who happen to live at the same address, to tell you the truth."

"So what's the question?" Bob said, sounding puzzled.

"Well, I just wondered why two people would marry and live together if they were so intent on remaining independent of one another in so many ways. I guess I'm so used to thinking like the Bible teaches, you know, that they are no longer two, but one. We share everything, and it seems like they share nothing. It just doesn't make much sense to me. Do you understand why people would marry and live that way? I mean, doesn't that almost defeat the whole purpose of being married?"

"I think it does, hon. And I can't tell you how glad I am that you think so."

From the Word

Unfortunately, the two-individuals-living-together style of marriage is more and more common. Pre-nuptial agreements, marriages of convenience, and open marriages all are modern distortions of the Biblical model. Christ presented the fundamental truth of marriage in Matthew 19:6 : "They are no longer two, but one." Any marriage which is simply a legal union of two individuals has missed the Biblical mark. The Biblical ideal is fulfilled when two people, without losing their unique personalities, gifts, and abilities, become one. It is, in fact, the purposeful blending of their individualism which gives the marriage union its strength. Independence decreases, as interdependence increases.

For the Heart

Stop and think of the way you and your spouse talk about the normal activities and business in your marriage and home. Make a list of the "I" and "we" areas as you usually describe them.

While all couples work out divisions of labor and activity which suit their marriage best, there is still room for examination. Are the "I" and "we" divisions based on convenience? Disagreement? Inability to find common ground?

Ask these questions about the "I" areas you discovered, and purpose to correct any disunity they reveal.

It takes hard work and conscious choices for two to become one.

DEVOTIONAL 5

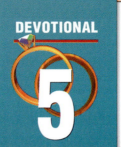

From Hurt to Hope

SCRIPTURE: Malachi 2:16

"For the Lord God of Israel says that He hates divorce, for it covers one's garment with violence," says the Lord of hosts. "Therefore take heed to your spirit, that you do not deal treacherously [with the wife of your youth]."

"I know you warned me about this before Larry and I split up," Lillith said to Pastor Burton. "But I guess I wasn't prepared for how it would haunt me—and now I don't know how to deal with it . . . with how I feel . . . and how I think God must feel about me . . ."

Wave after wave of soulish sobs pounded against the shore of Lillith's self-sufficiency. For months, her pent-up emotions had waged war with her conscience—trying to reach a truce, a peace of mind that would allow her to function.

Pastor Burton's secretary came in and sat with Lillith—holding her—providing for a moment the support that she had been unable to ask for.

"Lillith, I understand," Pastor Burton began. "The church family understands. Your own family understands. And most of all, God understands. I'm glad you came."

After a time of discussing with Lillith her fears, her guilt, her frustration over the twists and turns her life had taken, Pastor Burton felt Lillith needed to reach a point of closure with God about her divorce.

"Lillith, I think today could be a wonderful turning point in your life. Again, I am so glad you came. But I think you need to do something that maybe you've never done before."

"What?" Lillith sniffled.

"Agree with God that getting a divorce was wrong—*and be forgiven!* I know that He wants to forgive you and fill you with His hope for your future. The question is, 'Can you accept His forgiveness, and . . . forgive yourself?' "

From the Word

Pastor Burton is a wise counselor. Though hard, his words have their source in God's Word—and that is where wise counsel begins about marriage, and divorce.

God told a group of Israelite men, through the Prophet Malachi, that He hates divorce. The plain language in chapter three, verse sixteen, was meant to arrest their attention and hold it until they got the message. They were dealing treacherously with their wives. And He hated what they were doing. But God hates all sin, not just divorce. And for all sin, including divorce, there is cleansing and forgiveness, and hope for the future. The key is to agree *with* God, then receive *from* God.

For the Heart

Modern societies are filled with people who have divorced, and many who have remarried following divorce. Is this true of either you or your spouse? Or do you have a relative or close friend for whom this is true?

In helping yourself, or another, through healing after divorce, first be reconciled to God, calling divorce what He calls it, agreeing with His perspective. Then receive, and walk in, His unconditional love and forgiveness—with a clear conscience made possible by Christ's atoning death. His abundant grace and restoring love are just a decision away.

Though wounds may be deep, the healing grace of God is deeper.

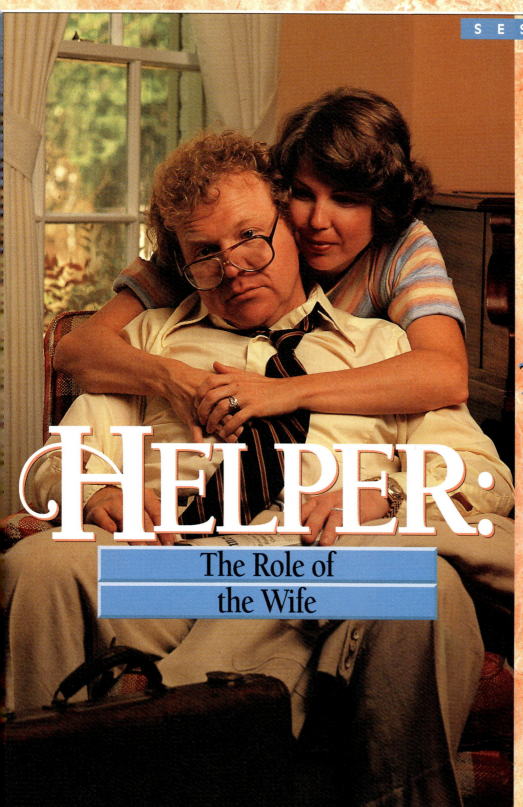

SESSION 3

HELPER:
The Role of the Wife

*T*he success of many a man is due to the helpfulness of his wife. Learn why the wife's honored role as helper to her husband is the foundation for a fruitful marital relationship. ■

CLASS NOTES

HELPER:
The Role of the Wife

INTRODUCTION

_____

_____

_____

From what possible sources might a wife get ideas about her role in marriage?

1. _____ … _____
2. _____ … _____
3. _____ … _____

_____

_____

How does the Bible define the role of the wife?

And the Lord God said, "It is not good that man should be alone; I will make him a _____ comparable to him" (Genesis 2:18).

_____

_____

3.2 A BIBLICAL PORTRAIT OF MARRIAGE   © 1995 by Dr. Bruce H. Wilkinson and Walk Thru the Bible Ministries, Inc. Do not reproduce.

In what ways is the wife to help her husband (Genesis 1:28)?

1. The wife is to help _____ _____ _____ of the husband.

2. The wife is to be a _____ to her husband (Genesis 1:26–27; 2:21; 1 Corinthians 11:3, 8–9, 11–12).

3. The husband is to _____ the help he needs.

_____
_____

CONCLUSION

EVALUATION

Helper: The Role of the Wife

Okay, it is time to do an evaluation in light of what was taught in this session. Think about the wife and her role as the helper in your marriage. With the perspectives of both husband and wife, the status of the wife's role will come more into focus.

The goal in these quizzes is to get the big picture regarding your marriage. It is not so much a snapshot of one day (or one incident during the day), but rather an overview of what is generally true at this time in your marriage.

Evaluate the wife's role as helper in your marriage. Total your score below.

		False			Sometimes			True
A	The wife consistently seeks to be a helper to her husband.	1	2	3	4	5	6	7
B	The husband is secure in his role as leader because his wife is not trying to fulfill that role herself.	1	2	3	4	5	6	7
C	The wife believes in her husband and enables him by her joyful and willing spirit.	1	2	3	4	5	6	7
D	An awareness of and familiarity with the husband's dreams and goals is one of the wife's highest priorities.	1	2	3	4	5	6	7
E	The wife frequently asks her husband what kind of help he needs or wants.	1	2	3	4	5	6	7
F	The wife finds delight in discovering how she can blend her strengths with her husband's in order to aid him in significant ways.	1	2	3	4	5	6	7
G	The husband experiences greater fulfillment of his dreams because of his wife's enablement and help.	1	2	3	4	5	6	7
H	The wife is happy and fulfilled in her role as helper to her husband.	1	2	3	4	5	6	7

Column Subtotals:

The Wife's "Helper" Score
- **48–56** "How may I help you?"
- **38–47** "I'll be right there, hon!"
- **28–37** "Maybe I should get you some help."
- **18–27** "Didn't I just help you with that?"
- **8–17** "Yeah, what do you want?"

GRAND TOTAL:

A BIBLICAL PORTRAIT OF MARRIAGE

© 1995 by Dr. Bruce H. Wilkinson and Walk Thru the Bible Ministries, Inc. Do not reproduce

INTERACTION

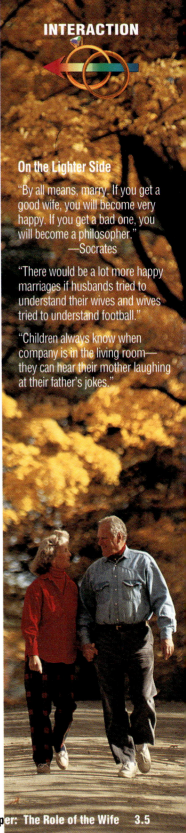

1 How has contemporary society defined the role of the wife? What has been the impact of this influence on the typical marriage?

2 Why are wives tempted at times to assume the leadership role in their marriages? How does such role reversal occur?

3 What are the characteristics of a wife who is *not* being a helper to her husband? What are some of the ways a husband might respond when his wife fails to support him in the fulfillment of his dreams?

4 What impact does a wife's attitude toward her role have on her husband? What might a husband do or say that would make it difficult for the wife to be a good helper?

5 What attitudes and behaviors have you observed in wives whom you perceive to be wonderful helpers to their husbands? What characterizes the husband of such a wife?

PROJECT: DETERMINE TO HELP

Is there an area in your marriage in which the husband desires help, but the wife is less than enthusiastic about giving it (and has not hesitated to make him aware of her feelings!)? Wife, **ask** your husband what area is most important to him and what specific help he desires. Then, **develop** a one-month strategy for fulfilling this particular request: week one, grin and bear it as you cover the basics; week two, add a creative touch; week three, suggest a few ways that you could possibly help even more; week four, discuss this area together and assess the progress. Then, get ready to celebrate!

On the Lighter Side

"By all means, marry. If you get a good wife, you will become very happy. If you get a bad one, you will become a philosopher."
—Socrates

"There would be a lot more happy marriages if husbands tried to understand their wives and wives tried to understand football."

"Children always know when company is in the living room—they can hear their mother laughing at their father's jokes."

BIBLE STUDY

HELPER

Equal in Value, But Not Equal Partners

Man and woman were both created in God's image. But when it came to marriage, God ordained the husband to lead and the wife to . . . help.

The roles of helping and leading are equally valued in Scripture. As you study these Scriptures, carefully consider how you should respond. Don't just be a "forgetful hearer," be a "doer" (James 1:22–25).

1 Helper by Design
Genesis 2:18–22

What kind of helper to the man did God design the woman to be?

What does it mean for a wife to complement or complete her husband?

In your marriage, what are several ways that the wife's personality, talents, and skills complement or complete the husband?

What does the husband most appreciate about the wife in her role as helper in your marriage?

In what one specific way could the wife be a better helper to her husband?

2 The Help Defined
Proverbs 12:4

Who defines whether the wife is helping in an excellent or shameful manner?

What reasons do many wives give for determining in their own minds what kind of help their husbands need?

Describe a time in your marriage when the wife helped the husband based upon what she thought he needed versus what he said he needed.

In your marriage, how does the husband respond when the wife provides help he didn't request or want?

In what specific ways would the wife's help be most valuable to the husband?

3.6 A BIBLICAL PORTRAIT OF MARRIAGE

© 1995 by Dr. Bruce H. Wilkinson and Walk Thru the Bible Ministries, Inc. Do not reproduce.

3 — A Worthy Helper
Proverbs 31:10–11

How does this husband feel toward his wife?

What are several characteristics of the husband who is convinced his wife is on his team?

Describe a challenging time in your marriage when the wife's trust made all the difference.

In what areas of your marriage does the husband wish the wife would exhibit more complete trust in him?

How could the wife express her trust in the husband more adequately?

4 — The Helper's Attitude
Proverbs 31:12–13

What is true of the wise wife in these verses?

What kind of impact does a wife's positive, willing attitude have on her husband?

In your marriage, what task does the wife do most willingly and which one does she fulfill somewhat grudgingly?

Why is it difficult in your marriage for the wife to exhibit a joyful and agreeable spirit toward the husband?

In what specific situations is the husband most frustrated by the wife's resistance and apparent unwillingness to help?

5 — Powerful Help
2 Corinthians 1:8–12

How did the Corinthian Christians help Paul in his time of trouble?

What benefits can a wife's prayers for her husband have in their marriage?

In your marriage, what hinders the wife from praying more consistently and fervently for the husband?

What are the three most important requests the husband would like his wife to pray for him?

Will you make every effort to cooperate with God's plan to ordain the wife as the helper to the husband in your marriage? Affirm your commitment to God by initialing and dating this page.

Your initials and date

Helper: The Role of the Wife

DEVOTIONAL 1

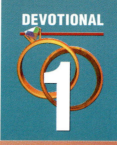

The Head of the Household

SCRIPTURE: Proverbs 31:10–31

She watches over the ways of her household, and does not eat the bread of idleness.

(verse 27)

Bob Ethridge, Sr., pulled Rick Winters aside after their Bible study. "Rick, how about going with me Saturday morning to the reservoir to haul in our share of bass?"

"I'd love to Bob, but you know how busy I've been with work lately. Saturday I've got to work half a day, and the other half I'm playing catch up at home with a 'to-do' list a mile long.

"By the way," Rick continued, "maybe this is a good time to ask you. How is it that you have time to do so many things, Bob? I mean, I know you're retired, but still—you and Alice always seem to have everything under control. No loose ends, no panics. Connie and I don't even have kids yet, and we can't seem to get everything done."

"Well," Bob smiled, throwing out some bait of his own, "come fishing with me Saturday and I'll tell you a secret Alice and I discovered that changed our marriage. It helps us get more done, and," he ended with an eye full of twinkle, "gave me more time for my bass conservation studies. Know what I mean?"

"Okay, I guess I'm hooked. But just for part of the afternoon."

Saturday, after getting settled in a "good spot" on the lake, Rick turned to Bob: "Okay professor, tell me this secret that's going to get Connie and me organized and put me on the lake four days a week."

"Well, it's actually just three days a week. Is that okay?"

"Very funny. To tell you the truth, once a month would be a start!"

From the Word

What do you think Bob and Alice had discovered in their marriage? Perhaps your marriage could benefit from their Scriptural secret. It is illustrated best in the Book of Proverbs, chapter 31, verse 27, where evidence of God's plan for husbands and wives is found. The couple in Proverbs 31 ran their marriage on a plan. The husband tended to his civic and vocational duties in the community (see verse 23) while the wife watched over the ways of her household (and they were diverse!). The wife serving as a helper to her husband reflects God's blueprint for building an effective marriage—each spouse knowing and fulfilling his or her role.

For the Heart

Wife, how are you fulfilling the role of helper to your husband? Are you comfortable with your role and responsibilities? On a piece of paper, make two columns: Clear and Confusing. Under each, list those areas of "helping" that you feel are clear between you and your husband, and those that could use some further discussion and definition. Show your lists to your husband and work together on your marriage's version of God's plan.

And husband—have you encouraged your wife "to be all that she can be" in light of Proverbs 31?

Husband: Head of the house.
Wife: Head of the "household."

3.8   A BIBLICAL PORTRAIT OF MARRIAGE   © 1995 by Dr. Bruce H. Wilkinson and Walk Thru the Bible Ministries, Inc. Do not reproduce.

Scriptural Helps for Helpers

DEVOTIONAL 2

SCRIPTURE: 2 Timothy 3:16

All Scripture is given by inspiration of God, and is profitable for doctrine, for reproof, for correction, for instruction in righteousness.

It was "Ladies Night Out" for the Ethridge clan. Grandmother Alice, her two daughters Betty and Lillith, daughter-in-law Deb, and Deb's thirteen-year-old daughter Kim were out on the town. Their monthly suppers together kept them in touch with each other and had been an Ethridge tradition for several years.

After gallant attempts to eat with chopsticks, they retreated to forks—and more focused conversation.

"Speaking of television, I saw an interesting thing the other day," Deb offered. "One of the daytime talk shows had a panel of women discussing whether wives should quit their jobs if their husband's job requires a move out of town. Or should the husband turn down his promotion or transfer, or whatever, and stay put so his wife could continue her career. Wow!—I was amazed at some of the answers!"

"Amazed at what, Deb?" Lillith asked. "That a wife's job could be just as important as the husband's? Or, heaven forbid, *more* important? A friend at the bank just went through that same thing, and gave up a very promising career to follow her husband across the country. I told her not to be afraid to suggest to her husband that he should give up his promotion so she could keep her job!"

"But Lillith," Betty responded, "that's so arbitrary. Marriage would be nothing but a series of negotiations and power plays if both the husband and wife are expecting the other to follow!"

"Where does the Bible say the wife has to quit her job?" Lillith asked.

From the Word

Don't spend a long time looking for that verse! Scriptural guidance for specific personal situations—such as Lillith is asking for—is rarely found. Instead, consider 2 Timothy 3:16, which says that Scripture is profitable for instruction. That is, we know Scripture clearly says that the wife is to be the helper of the husband—not the other way around. In marriage, therefore, as in other leader/follower settings, when the leader moves, the helpers follow. Are there exceptions? Of course. A loving husband should take his wife's desires into serious consideration, and possibly even change his plans. But the *first* step is always, "Am I willing to follow the general Scriptural guidelines for my role in marriage?"

For the Heart

Wife, can you think of a situation recently where you disagreed with your husband's plans for your marriage or family? Was your concern over immorality or illegality? Marital disagreements rarely are of that nature. They are usually about personal preferences or opinions, aren't they?

If necessary, perhaps you could talk with your husband about your disagreement, and reaffirm your desire to help him—even if you disagree, and even if he is wrong!

Husbands, are you willing to hear your wife's point of view?

The first principles to obey are the ones we know today.

DEVOTIONAL 3

Two for the Call of One

SCRIPTURE
Ephesians 5:21

[Submit] to one another in the fear of God.

"Bob," Alice called to her husband, "John called while you were out and asked if he could drop by for a few minutes tonight to talk. He said he had something important to discuss."

Bob stopped in the middle of the kitchen floor without putting the groceries down. *Pastor Lawrence? I wonder what he wants?* Bob thought to himself. "Okay—I'll be here. Guess I've been singing louder than I thought," Bob called to his wife.

"No comment," came the safe reply.

Later that evening, after cake and coffee, Pastor Lawrence loosened his tie and sat up on the edge of his chair. The time had come.

"Bob and Alice, after a lot of prayer and thought—and the counsel of your peers—I've come to ask Bob for his permission to be nominated to serve as chairman of our church's board for the next two-year term. I wanted to discuss this with both of you because you know that at Grace Church this is a position of great responsibility. In the past, it has usually absorbed a large portion of the time of *both* husband and wife."

After another hour of discussion about the chairman's position, and their role as a couple, Bob and Alice promised to give the pastor a response within a week.

And until late that night, Bob thought prayerfully about Alice's comment when the pastor was there: "I guess this means I'd have to give up my ministry at the nursing home—if you take the position—right?" He knew she was right. The board's chairman position would dominate their lives.

From the Word

In this situation, does the role of helper mean that Alice should do what Bob is asked to do? Ultimately, yes. But a godly husband will always want to make sure that he has sought and understood God's will before making a decision. And Ephesians 5:21 gives good direction for this initial step. Perhaps Bob would suggest, "Alice, for starters, let's both release our desires—first to each other, then to the Lord. He will somehow tell us whether I should take this new ministry position—or not." Alice might reply: "Good idea. Ultimately, I want to do what God wants us to do. And I appreciate you being willing to give Him the opportunity to confirm this opportunity—or not."

For the Heart

In the wake of the modern women's movement, the above scenario may seem unlikely. How about to you as a wife? Does it seem outdated or unrealistic? Perhaps a fresh consideration today of your role as your husband's helper will give you a new perspective.

The next time you and your husband face a decision with opposite interests, consider this: If you sense that God is clearly calling your husband in a new direction, would He not also be calling your husband's helper as well (don't look now, but that's you!)?

God is efficient: His plan allows one call to serve for both.

DEVOTIONAL 4

All Women Are Not Wives

SCRIPTURE
Galatians 3:28

There is neither Jew nor Greek, there is neither slave nor free, there is neither male nor female; for you are all one in Christ Jesus.

Focused on the sports page at breakfast, Bob was only slightly tuned in to the instructions Bobby was laying out for his sister, Kim, that Monday morning:

"...and because I've got a big algebra test tomorrow I'd really appreciate it if you'd do my dishes after supper. And could you put a lunch together for me for tomorrow? Uh, ham sandwich—no mustard, please—dill pickle, chips, an apple, and...a surprise. Well, I need to get going."

"Whoa, whoa, Bobby!" Bob interjected, looking like a traffic cop ready to stop a fleeing thief. Turning to Deb, who was poised with spatula in midair and a "who-invited-the-dictator-to-breakfast?" look on her face, Bob asked, "What is this all about, Deb? Kim doing dishes and making lunch for Bobby?"

A bewildered shrug of her shoulders was all Deb could muster, so Bob turned to his son, still standing tall and looking confident—like maybe eliminating the national debt before lunch wouldn't be that hard.

"Bobby, what gives?" Bob asked, his rising impatience causing Bobby's confidence to dissipate. "Since when is your sister your servant?"

"Well, you know, Dad. Pastor Kallan said in church yesterday how God made the woman to be the helper of the man, and so it seems like it might be good for Kim and me to start practicing—I can learn to ask for help, and she can learn to give it! It makes perfect sense!"

Bobby's confidence had returned. He knew this was a great idea.

From the Word

Bobby was a bit unclear on the concept, don't you think? Unfortunately, some husbands believe and practice Bobby's (per)version of the truth. To be a helper is not to be a slave. And to be a woman is not to be a helper to all men. When God created man and woman, He created them with equal standing in His sight, as Galatians 3:28 shows. Women were not created to serve men. Rather, wives were appointed to help their husbands. The difference is significant. In marriage, any husband who believes his wife is his servant has misread Scripture. And any man who believes women in general are to serve men has likewise erred—and will likely be promptly told!

For the Heart

Wife, has your husband ever treated you more like a servant than he has honored you as a helper? What was your response? If you have stored up any anger at all, will you confess it to the Lord today? God understands your feelings, but wants you to commit them to Him, lest they cause your marriage harm in the future.

Forgive your husband, and then plan a time to talk over this issue—with your pastor's help if necessary.

Husband, if you have treated your wife like a servant rather than a helper, will you apologize? Today would be a great day to ask for—not demand!—her forgiveness.

Men who seek a servant instead of a wife seek in vain.

DEVOTIONAL 5

Honor Where It's Due

SCRIPTURE
Proverbs 31:28b

Her husband also,
. . . praises her.

"As is usual each year," the president began his remarks, "the shift managers and section leaders from the whole plant voted for the Manager of the Year. And this year, Bob Ethridge, Jr., has won in a landslide!"

"Wow! What a surprise, Pete," Bob said, shaking hands with the president after making his way to the podium. "I had no idea!"

When the applause subsided, Bob looked at his plaque, his new gold watch, the audience—and found Deb's eyes. He took a deep breath. *Here goes, Lord.*

"Well, first of all, let's get one thing clear—I'm a manager, not an after-dinner speaker. So bear with me a moment," Bob laughed nervously. "I do appreciate this award, more than you know. But there's another person who should be up with me taking much of the credit. Let me explain," he said to the puzzled faces staring at him.

"Pete—" Bob continued, looking at the president, "and all of you—you need to know who makes it possible for me to show up on time, wear socks that match, eat a healthy lunch instead of a candy bar, and explains overtime to the kids when I'm not home on Saturday—and, well, you men know what I'm talking about.

"Since being promoted to shift supervisor two years ago, there's a lot more to think about. And to be honest, I'm able to keep a clear head and keep thoughts focused at work because I know that things at home are so well taken care of. And for that, you all need to thank my wife, Deb—sitting right over there."

From the Word

"Wow! What a surprise," said the readers. "We had no idea there were men like that out there!"

Granted, it would take a noble and strong man to stand up in public and give praise to his wife. But Scripture records, in Proverbs 31:28, another husband who did so thousands of years ago. What would make a man do such a thing? Probably, as in Proverbs 31, the absolute magnitude of his wife's helpfulness to him in life. Some things just have to be said! When a wife makes her husband's life a success through her stability, skill, and sensitive partnering—that is, her helpfulness—it is hard to keep it in. Be it ancient times or modern, the truth is hard to hide!

For the Heart

Wife, at the conclusion of these devotionals on your role as your husband's helper, let's take stock. Jot down two or three areas that come to mind in which you know you are significantly helping your husband. Thank God for those!

And would you consider this long-term prayer? Ask God to one day allow your husband to praise his helper in public—NOT for your credit, but for your personal confirmation that God has opened up new dimensions of success as you fulfill His role for your life.

Husbands: See below!

Those who honor others will likely receive honor themselves.

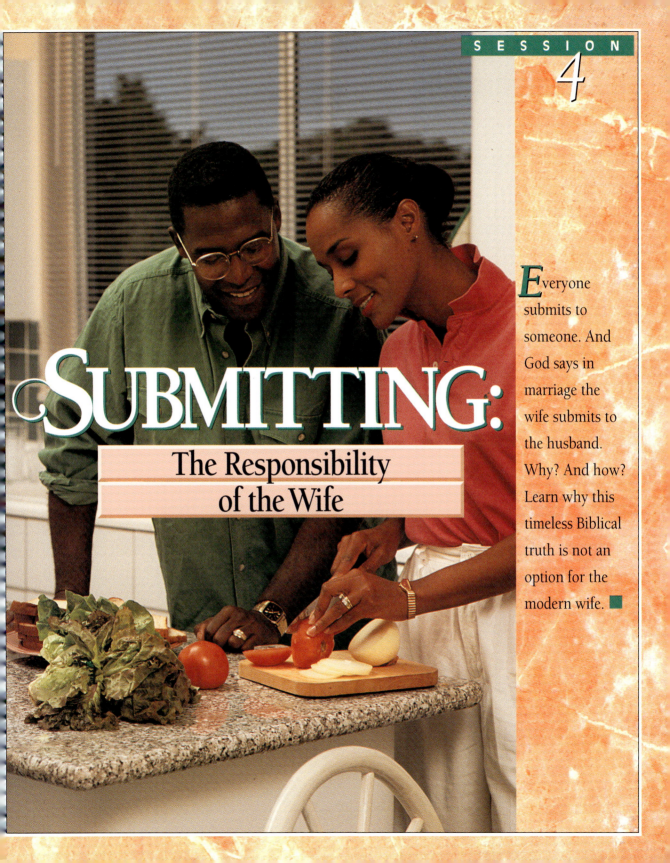

SESSION 4

SUBMITTING:
The Responsibility of the Wife

*E*veryone submits to someone. And God says in marriage the wife submits to the husband. Why? And how? Learn why this timeless Biblical truth is not an option for the modern wife.

CLASS NOTES

SUBMITTING:

The Responsibility of the Wife

INTRODUCTION

_____

_____

_____

  hat are the key Biblical passages concerning the wife's responsibility to submit to her husband?

1. _____   3. _____

2. _____

  hat is the nature of Biblical submission for the wife in the marriage?

1. Submission means the wife is to _____ _____ underneath her husband.

2. The wife's submission to her husband is an _____ command.

3. The wife is to submit _____ to her husband.

_____

_____

What are the seven characteristics of a Biblically submissive wife?

1. Wives are to submit to their _____ _____ (Colossians 3:18).

2. It is _____, it is _____, for the wife to submit to her own husband (Colossians 3:18).

3. The wife is to submit with _____ as the church does to Christ (Ephesians 5:22–24).

4. The wife is to submit to her husband in _____ (Ephesians 5:24).

5. The wife is to submit by her conduct, _____ _____ _____ (1 Peter 3:1).

6. Submission is to be accompanied by _____ or very strong respect (1 Peter 3:2).

7. The wife is to submit with a _____ and _____ spirit (1 Peter 3:3–4).

CONCLUSION

_____

_____

Submitting: The Responsibility of the Wife 4.3

EVALUATION

Submitting: The Responsibility of the Wife

It can be very difficult to assess how you are doing in a given area of life—especially an emotional and relational area like marriage. So do your best to be as objective as possible in light of what is generally true.

Use these evaluation points much as you would a compass. First, get your bearings—assess where you are in relation to where you need to go. Then focus your efforts with renewed purpose toward God's goals for your marriage.

How is the wife fulfilling her responsibility to submit to her own husband? Total your score below.

		False		Sometimes				True
A	The wife has voluntarily placed herself in submission to her husband.	1	2	3	4	5	6	7
B	The wife finds joy in submission and does not chafe at or resist God's command to submit to her husband.	1	2	3	4	5	6	7
C	Outside of breaking civil or Biblical law, there is no area in which the wife is unwilling to submit to her husband.	1	2	3	4	5	6	7
D	The wife has learned to submit to her husband even when she feels he is wrong.	1	2	3	4	5	6	7
E	When the wife feels her husband is wrong, she appeals to him in a way that is neither demeaning nor contentious.	1	2	3	4	5	6	7
F	The wife's godly character and manner of life are persuasive without her saying a single word.	1	2	3	4	5	6	7
G	The wife boasts about her husband to others and consistently portrays him in a positive fashion.	1	2	3	4	5	6	7
H	Even though the husband is an imperfect man, he is confident that his wife respects him in his office as leader.	1	2	3	4	5	6	7

Column Subtotals:

The Wife's "Submitting" Score
- **48–56** Wife submits on days that end in "y."
- **38–47** Submits on odd-numbered days only.
- **28–37** "I'll do it. Just don't tell me when!"
- **18–27** Patriotic—submits on all national holidays.
- **8–17** "What part of 'NO' don't you understand?"

GRAND TOTAL:

INTERACTION

1 Why is submission such a volatile issue in today's society? What can make it difficult for a wife to submit to her husband?

2 When a husband "forces" his wife to submit, what is the potentially negative impact on her personality and emotions?

3 What is at the heart of God's command that wives submit to their husbands? What characterizes the wife who submits *herself* to her husband?

4 When a wife is unwilling to submit herself to her husband, what are the consequences—to her, to her husband, and to their marriage?

5 How could a wife's perspective be affected by realizing that when she submits to her husband she is actually submitting to God?

On the Lighter Side

"When a man and a woman marry they become one—and they spend the rest of their lives trying to find out which one."

"Two Texas political candidates were having a heated debate. One shouted, 'What about the power interests that control you?' The other screamed back, 'You leave my wife out of this.'"

"When a man decides to marry, it may be the last decision he'll ever be allowed to make."

PROJECT: RESOLVE TO SUBMIT

Identify some of the reasons why the wife might struggle in submitting to the husband in your marriage. Does the struggle arise from the past? An unhealthy experience in another arena? A lack of respect for the husband (generally or in a specific area)? Is it anything more than flesh rebelling against authority? Whatever it is, wives, **commit** yourself before the Lord to **submit** to your husband as unto the Lord the next time you experience this struggle. **Repeat** this process as needed. Then **evaluate**—is submission getting any easier? And husbands, **strategize** how you might make it easier for your wife to submit to you.

BIBLE STUDY

The "S" Word

Submission. The very word can instantly bring a look of intense anger or cowering fear to the face of a wife. In a few rare instances, a wife might find herself responding with a gentle smile. Few other fundamental issues in marriage stir the intensity of response that this issue generates.

God's Word is clear in the instruction given regarding submission— for wives, children, employees, and all believers. In these studies, both husband and wife will benefit from the clear principles presented in the Word of God about submission.

1 Submission's Extent
Ephesians 5:22–24

To what extent are wives to submit to their own husbands?

As you think of the typical marriage, what percentage of the time does the wife submit to her husband?

In your marriage, what hinders the wife from submitting to the husband in everything?

In what specific area of your marriage would the wife's submission mean the most to the husband?

2 Submission's School
Hebrews 5:5–8

What impact did suffering have on Christ's obedience?

What are some of the emotions a wife might experience in the process of learning obedience as it relates to submission?

In your marriage, give an example of a time when the wife obeyed the husband, although it was very difficult at the time.

How has the wife learned obedience so far in your marriage?

3 Submission's Power
1 Peter 5:5–7

What character quality is closely associated with submission in this passage?

How does a humble person speak and act?

In what areas of your marriage does the wife struggle with pride or the need to prove she is right?

How have you experienced God's grace when you humbled yourself in your marriage?

In what aspect of your marriage would a humble spirit have the greatest impact?

4 Submission's Conduct
1 Peter 3:1–6

How is a wife to show submission to the husband?

Describe the conduct of a godly wife.

In your marriage, what aspects of the wife's behavior are the most winsome and attractive to the husband?

At this time, in what area of your marriage should the wife trust God rather than attempt to verbally influence the husband?

5 Submission's Honor
Ephesians 5:33

What key word in this passage summarizes how a wife is to relate to her husband?

How does a husband respond when his wife expresses her honor and respect for him?

In your marriage, what does the wife respect the most about her husband?

In what aspect of your marriage would the wife's demonstration of respect for the husband make the greatest difference to him?

Will you commit yourself to honor and elevate the wife's responsibility to submit to her husband in your marriage? Affirm your commitment by initialing and dating this page.

Your initials and date

DEVOTIONAL 1

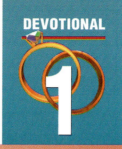

Everybody Obeys Somebody

SCRIPTURE: Matthew 8:5–13

The only thing rising faster than Lillith's blood pressure was the speedometer needle on her BMW.

"Where does Larry get off calling me like that?" she fumed. "He knew I needed him to take Allison today—but no, 'Something's come up.' Why I ever married someone who thinks it's his constitutional right to be in charge, I'll never know. At least I was in charge during our divorce!"

After the early-Sunday-morning call from Larry, Lillith calmed down enough to dress Allison and head for church. But as she mentally replayed his phone call, her high-octane anger turned her car into an invitation for a ticket. From out of nowhere, a policeman materialized in her mirror—another man just waiting to lord it over her.

Give me a break! Why isn't this guy in church or out catching drug dealers? she thought as she pulled to the side of the road.

She stood, sang, sat, prayed, greeted, and contributed her way through the first half of the service, oblivious to it all. It took her that long to process through both of her male-induced put-downs that morning. Larry and a cop. Larry is like a cop. All men are like . . .

"Turn with me to Matthew, chapter eight," intruded yet a third male—Pastor Dan Burton. "We'll continue our sermon series on husbands and wives this morning by looking at Jesus and a Roman centurion."

A Roman centurion, Lillith thought. *What's that got to do with marriage?*

The centurion . . . said, " . . . For I also am a man under authority, having soldiers under me. And I say to this one, 'Go,' and he goes; and to another, 'Come,' and he comes; and to my servant, 'Do this,' and he does it."

(verses 8–9)

From the Word

Indeed! What does a Roman centurion have to do with marriage? In Matthew 8, when Christ meets this man, He is overwhelmed by the soldier's faith—and his understanding of a key principle in the kingdom of God: Authority. Like it or not, everyone is under someone's authority! Whether in the state, in the church, or in marriage, God has His authority structures.

Though Lillith had wrestled with submitting to her husband—and with authority figures in general—she was not the first to wrestle with this issue. God's ordered structures often run counter to cultural norms, but they are His way of blessing and protecting His people.

For the Heart

Wives, regardless of your practice in submitting to your husband, you can probably identify with Lillith. All of us struggle with submission. It is against our human nature to "give in" to another.

Wife, is there a particularly challenging area in which it is difficult to submit to your husband? And husband, are your desires for your wife's submission sometimes conveyed inappropriately? As we begin this week of devotions on submission, would you pray for your ability to respond positively to God, to His Word, and to your spouse?

How to impress Jesus Christ: Live joyfully under authority.

DEVOTIONAL 2

Winning Without a Word

SCRIPTURE
1 Peter 3:1–4

Likewise you wives, be submissive to your own husbands, that even if some do not obey the word, they, without a word, may be won by the conduct of their wives.

(verse 1)

"Alice!" Bob, Sr., barked as he marched purposefully into the kitchen, interrupting Alice and Deb's conversation.

"I just looked at the mileage on your car. You were due for an oil change and lube 600 miles ago! I have asked you to please watch the mileage and let me know when it's due. That's what the little sticker on the windshield is for! Good grief, Alice—an oil change is a whole lot less expensive than a new car!"

Bob's back was all the reply Alice got as she tried to respond: "Bob, I'm sorry. You're right. I've been meaning to tell you . . ."

Deb wasn't sure what to say. She hadn't seen her father-in-law that angry very often. Alice looked genuinely hurt.

"I know how you must feel, Alice. I'd be hurt, too. You ought to go talk to him about treating you that way!"

Alice was quiet for a moment before replying. She knew she stood at a fork in the road. Down one way was the fleshly satisfaction of reprimanding Bob for the way he spoke to her, especially in front of Deb. And down the other lay the Biblical way, where she knew she would encounter the kingdom of God. She couldn't fail Deb, Bob—and God—by choosing amiss.

"Yes, Deb, I think I am going to talk to Bob. I'm going to tell him—gently and quietly—that I'm sorry for not doing what he asked me to do. I believe I'll win my best friend back sooner that way."

"But, Alice . . ."

"No buts, Deb. God says a quiet spirit is needed at a time like this."

From the Word

Was Alice right? When faced with a demonstration of carnality, is meekness God's will? Absolutely!

First Peter 3:1–4 is one of the clearest passages in Scripture on the "how" and "why" to respond to a husband's sin. And it is provided for wives. While Peter may have written this passage originally to address wives whose husbands had not yet become believers—and definitely were still living like it!—the principles apply to wives with believing husbands as well.

The "how" is to let the gentleness and quietness of your spirit totally surround your response. No preaching, no nagging, no retaliating. Why? Because your life will be a living example of love—exactly what is needed by a carnal husband.

For the Heart

A frequent response of wives to Peter's exhortation is, "I've tried it. It doesn't work!" That would be like a farmer saying, "I planted my seed this morning. Where's my corn?" Give God time! When you respond gently and quietly, trust God—things are happening! Your husband is aware of his mistakes, and your love makes it more likely that he will change. Plan now to be gentle and quiet when the next storm comes ashore.

Husbands, now that you know your wife's secret weapon, don't be defensive! She'll just be gentler and quieter still!

The mightiest song is often sung by the softest voice.

Submitting: The Responsibility of the Wife   4.9

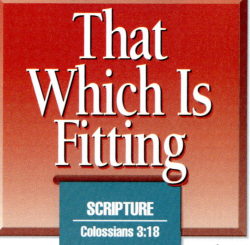

DEVOTIONAL 3

That Which Is Fitting

SCRIPTURE: Colossians 3:18

Wives, submit to your own husbands, as is fitting in the Lord.

The Thursday night Bible study at Betty's house had grown to almost a dozen energetic young women—all single.

After opening in prayer, and before she could even begin her lesson, a question was launched:

"Betty, I met Mr. Right today at work," Amy gushed. "No, I mean it," she continued, trying to talk over the group's ribbing. "I need to know tonight—what do I have to do to prepare to get married—next week? This is really it! I know it!"

Betty was trying to separate the wheat from the chaff in Amy's question. While this lively young lady could be the life of any party, Betty sensed a serious inquiry lurking beneath her lighthearted manner.

"Well, Amy, you never cease to keep us on our toes. Should we mark our calendars? Not yet? Good, because the answer to your question is going to take more than a week.

"And here it is: The best way for any woman to prepare to marry is to learn to submit herself to God. In good times, bad times, testing times, regular times—all the time. You must learn to submit to Him—and joyfully."

"That's it?" Amy asked. "I don't think I get the connection."

"Let me explain. Your chief responsibility in marriage is to submit to your husband, and to do it 'as is fitting in the Lord,' Scripture says. That means, you are to submit to your husband as an expression of your submission to the Lord. Therefore, the best way to learn to submit to your husband 'next week' is to submit to the Lord 'this week!'"

From the Word

When Paul wrote to the Colossians, he was imparting a Christian "world view" that would shape all of their daily relationships. Christian people should give evidence of their faith. For a wife, the norm is to submit to her husband. Why? Because God's appointed leader in marriage is the husband, and to submit to the husband is for the wife a way of saying, "God, I honor You, and Your plan for marriage, by complying with it." In other words, wives should submit because it is fitting if they are "in the Lord," meaning if they are Christians. To submit to the husband is to demonstrate a spirit of submissiveness to the Lord. A lack of submission would show the opposite.

For the Heart

Are there not plenty of other ways that a wife can manifest the lordship of Christ? Certainly there are, but none so important as submitting to her husband.

Not only is submission the most important, it is also one of the *hardest* things for a wife to do—but, one of the most productive. Wife, take a minute to sit down with your husband and ask, "Is there any way that my submissiveness to you, or the lack of it, lessens your respect for my Christian life?" If the answer is "Yes," hear out your husband, and take his comments to heart—and to the Lord, if needed.

How to "fit in" with the Lord? Submit to your husband!

DEVOTIONAL 4

What Jesus Didn't Do

SCRIPTURE
1 Peter 2:21–23

Who, when He was reviled, did not revile in return; when He suffered, He did not threaten, but committed Himself to Him who judges righteously.

(verse 23)

"Hi, hon! Ooooh—I love it! You're fixing my favorite supper! Liver and onions—I could smell 'em in the driveway! Way to go, Deb! Deb? What's wrong? I know liver and onions isn't your favorite, but it's not that bad is it?" teased Bob, Jr.

"No, I'm sorry. I've just felt down all afternoon—discouraged, I guess."

"Why?"

"Well, you know the lady we met in Sunday School—the one that just moved here from up north? Beverly Landers?"

"I remember."

"Well, I dropped by her house this afternoon just to visit, and I learned more about her than we did Sunday. And some of it was pretty sad."

"Like what? She doesn't fix liver and onions for her husband?"

"Bob, this is serious. She probably would do that, or anything else he asked, if he would treat her better. I don't think he's a Christian—I wondered why she was in church alone—and apparently he treats her pretty badly at times."

"What do you mean?"

"Well, lots of verbal abuse, name calling—and I think when he drinks it gets pretty offensive at times. She was pretty careful about what she said, but I can tell it's serious. Her eyes welled up with tears while we talked. She said she didn't know what to do."

"Wow! So what did you tell her?"

Deb looked at Bob with her eyes brimming. "The same thing Pastor Kallan told me about how to respond to my mom's need to control. Follow Jesus' example, first and foremost, because God is a righteous judge."

From the Word

What Deb told Beverly Landers, and what Pastor Kallan had told her, is based on 1 Peter 2:21–23. It is unfortunate, but true, that some wives at times find themselves in situations requiring their "non-retaliation." As Peter explains, when Christ was reviled, hurt, and made to suffer by others, he did not return the words or actions to His tormentors. Rather He "committed Himself to" (that is, submitted Himself to the will of) God whom He knew would judge righteously one day. The temptation for a wife to strike back, to lash out, and to seek revenge is great—and understandable. But, like Christ, wives must stay committed to their heavenly Father who knows their condition and needs.

For the Heart

When was the last time you retaliated against your husband with an unkind word or action? And how recently did you submit yourself to him—and to God—and choose not to return the unkindness? Which of the two responses is most consistent in your life?

If it is the former, could you pause for a moment and yield your heart and will to God? Could you pray, "Father, I commit myself to a non-retaliating relationship with my husband. I want to be like Christ."

Husbands, would you spare your wife the temptation to do otherwise?

What one doesn't do is often as important as what one does.

DEVOTIONAL 5

What Does Everything Mean?

SCRIPTURE
Ephesians 5:24

Therefore, just as the church is subject to Christ, so let the wives be to their own husbands in everything.

Betty's best friend in the world, Sarah Randall, had stopped by to visit. No one could listen like Sarah, and when Betty's husband died, she and Betty spent long hours talking and praying together.

"So, what did you get Jack for his birthday, Sarah?" Betty asked over tea.

When Sarah's eyes fell, Betty's radar went off.

"Did something happen? Sarah? . . ."

"Well, I had this special fishing 'thing'—a rod and reel, whatever—picked out. Jack had it circled in a catalog. He really wanted it— and I'd been saving for it. But it was really expensive, and when it came time to order it I didn't have enough money to write a check—you know how tight things have been for us lately—and so I charged it on my credit card. I thought I could save the rest of the money before the bill came and get it paid off. No problem, right?

"But then, when Jack unwrapped it, and he knew how much it cost, the accountant in him started asking questions, and I finally had to tell him I had charged it. Since things have been so tight financially he had asked me not to use my credit card, and I had agreed. And we both had stopped using them.

"But then I just couldn't help it. I think I was more concerned about being embarrassed at not having a nice gift than I was about doing what he asked. Anyway, it sort of deflated the whole birthday thing. And, he sent it back."

"Wow! Makes for a bad party, huh?" Betty sympathized.

"Did it ever! I just didn't think it was so important. But I guess I was wrong."

From the Word

Was Sarah wrong? What do you think? Her intent was good—to do something nice for her husband. But her method was flawed. While the Bible does not say "do not use credit cards," it does say, "Wives submit to your husbands in everything." When the Apostle Paul penned those words (Ephesians 5:24), could he have meant *everything*? We must assume so, since that is what the text says.

The issue at stake is one of Biblical principles. Just as we are not free to pick one "small" Biblical command to violate, neither are we free to violate the instructions of one of His ordained authorities. It can make for more than just a "bad party."

For the Heart

As a tiny pebble in a shoe can make walking unbearable, so a small indiscretion against authority can take the joy out of that relationship.

Wife, is there any small pebble of dishonor in your husband's shoe because of your lack of submission on some occasion? What would it take to remove it? Perhaps this week—even today—would be the perfect time to talk with him. Will you ask God's forgiveness, and then your husband's? He will walk with you easier if you do.

Husband—be receptive! The shoe may be on her foot next time.

Submitting in everything means submitting in EVERY thing.

SESSION 5

LEADER:
The Role of the Husband

When God calls people together for any purpose, He also designates a leader to be responsible for them and direct their activities. Discover God's clear direction for the husband to be the leader of the wife. ■

LEADER: The Role of the Husband

INTRODUCTION

_____

_____

_____

_____

From God's perspective, the husband is the _____ in the marriage (Genesis 2:15–18; 3:16; Ephesians 5:22–24).

_____

_____

Why don't husbands lead?

1. Wrong Beliefs

   I don't _____ _____ to lead.

   I don't feel _____ _____ to lead.

   I'm not _____ _____ to lead.

   _____

   _____

2. Wrong Behaviors

   _____

   _____

   _____

   _____

   _____

LEADER How do wives want their husbands to lead?

By being the . . .

1. _____   5. _____

2. _____   6. _____

3. _____   7. _____

4. _____

_____

_____

CONCLUSION (1 Timothy 3:1, 4–5)

_____

_____

_____

_____

EVALUATION

Leader: The Role of the Husband

In this quiz, think about the husband and his role as the leader of the wife. Both the husband's and the wife's perspectives will be valuable in assessing the state of leadership in your marriage.

Remember: This is not a test, and your resulting score is not a grade. Rather, let these evaluation points stimulate your thinking about how these truths are being applied in your marriage.

Evaluate the office of husband as leader in your marriage. Total your score below.

		False			Sometimes			True
A	The husband is comfortable as the ruler, leader, and initiator in the marriage.	1	2	3	4	5	6	7
B	The husband is growing in his knowledge and understanding of how to be a leader to his wife.	1	2	3	4	5	6	7
C	Confidence and security characterize the husband when leading the marriage.	1	2	3	4	5	6	7
D	When obstacles arise, the husband reacts actively and energetically, not passively.	1	2	3	4	5	6	7
E	The wife feels secure, safe, and protected by her husband.	1	2	3	4	5	6	7
F	The husband provides for the family's financial needs without depending on additional income from the wife.	1	2	3	4	5	6	7
G	One of the husband's highest priorities is promoting spiritual growth as a couple.	1	2	3	4	5	6	7
H	The husband gives tender comfort to his wife when she is ill, is under stress, or is emotionally hurt.	1	2	3	4	5	6	7

Column Subtotals:

The Husband's "Leader" Score
- **48–56** Five-Star Leader.
- **38–47** CHAR-R-R-GE!
- **28–37** Looking for the battle plan.
- **18–27** "Have you seen my white flag anywhere?"
- **8–17** A.W.O.L. (Absent WithOut Leading).

GRAND TOTAL:

1 What factors in today's society contribute to a distorted view of the husband's leadership in marriage?

2 What are the differences between "passive" leadership and "pro-active" leadership? From marriages you have observed, give an illustration of each of these two styles.

3 Why do some husbands at times grow passive in leading their wives? What impact does this have on the emotions and motivations of both the husband and wife?

4 What have you observed a wife doing that discouraged her husband from leading? What could she have done to encourage her husband to be the leader in their marriage?

5 What are some factors that tend to intimidate a husband in the area of spiritual leadership? What would help a husband to demonstrate more initiative in leading his wife spiritually?

PROJECT: LEARN TO LEAD

Write down the seven roles of a leader mentioned in this session—Protector, Provider, Scout, General, Priest, Physician, and King. **Star** the role in which the husband excels. (Wives, congratulate your husband for his success in this role!) **Circle** the specific role you both think is most needful at this time in your marriage. **Discuss** your answers together. Husbands, **describe** the way you will exercise leadership in the area your wife indicated was needful. Wives, **specify** the way you will encourage and support your husband in this venture.

INTERACTION

On the Lighter Side

"A man in Oklahoma admitted he lied on his income tax return—he listed himself as head of the household!"

"When a man says, 'I run things at my house,' he may mean the washing machine, the vacuum cleaner, and the furnace."

BIBLE STUDY

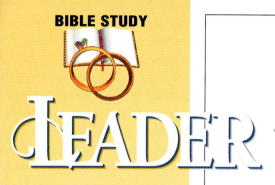

LEADER

Who Put *Him* in Charge?

The fact is—*God* did. And what an exciting and awesome challenge it is!

Do not allow yourself to be overwhelmed in this task. Do not give in to any fear of failure. And do not get angry at God for ordaining the husband as the leader in marriage.

Do ask God for wisdom. Do search the Scriptures for help. And do commit yourself to apply these principles in your own life and marriage— even today.

1 Leadership by Design — Ephesians 5:23

What role is the husband designated to fill in marriage?

List at least three areas in which a husband should lead his wife.

Who would your friends say is usually the leader in your marriage?

Why would they say that?

What is the one area in your marriage in which the husband needs to lead the wife more effectively?

2 A Bold Leader — Genesis 12:1–5

What instruction did Abraham immediately obey that had a radical impact on Sarah's life?

In what types of difficult and challenging situations does a husband need to lead with boldness?

What bold step of leadership has the husband taken in your marriage that was tough for him, but right for the family?

In what area is it particularly difficult for the husband to exercise leadership right now in your marriage?

What steps of action do you believe Abraham would advise the husband to take in the face of this challenge?

3. A Role Surrendered
Genesis 16:1–6

In Genesis 13:16, what did God promise Abraham?

In Genesis 16, how did Abraham surrender leadership to Sarah?

Name three situations which tempt a husband to surrender leadership to his wife.

Has the husband surrendered leadership to the wife at any time in your marriage? If so, give an example.

How could the husband avoid this mistake in the future?

4. Ruling as a Role
1 Timothy 3:4–5, 12

What reputation is a godly husband to have in relation to his family?

What types of behaviors have you observed in men who seem to be good leaders in their marriages?

Identify several ways the husband fulfills his role as the leader in your marriage.

What needs to be changed or enhanced in order for the husband to be seen more clearly as the leader in your marriage?

5. The Spiritual Leader
Job 1:1–5

How did Job exercise spiritual leadership in his home?

What are at least three things a contemporary husband could do to be a spiritual leader to his wife?

What are the greatest hindrances the husband faces in being the spiritual leader of the home?

In your marriage, what is the most important thing the husband could do at this time to lead his wife spiritually?

Will you honor God's plan to establish the husband as the leader in your marriage? Signify your commitment by initialing and dating this page.

Your initials and date

Leader: The Role of the Husband   5.7

DEVOTIONAL 1

The Soul Purpose of Leadership

SCRIPTURE
Hebrews 13:7, 17

Obey those who rule over you ... for they watch out for your souls, as those who must give account. Let them do so with joy and not with grief, for that would be unprofitable for you.

(verse 17)

Bob knew that when his 70-year-old dad offered to come over and work on a "project" that there was more at stake than just repairs. Bob, Jr.'s, pickup was about to become the senior Bob's podium.

"Son, you know I try to keep my distance when it comes to your family. I know it's not my place to interfere," began Bob, Sr.

"But . . ." his son grinned.

"I guess you know me pretty well, huh? Okay, I'll just say it. When your mother and I were over for dinner the other night, I noticed some video movies stacked on the VCR that I was a bit surprised to see in your house. I know you don't watch that many movies, so I assume they were Deb's or the kids'. Well, some of them looked pretty marginal—you know, maybe some questionable content.

"I guess I wondered if you knew what movies were in that stack. Are you keeping up with what your family is watching these days? Is it good stuff—consistent with their spiritual development and all?

"Here's my point, Bob. At the church elders' meeting recently, we looked at a verse—Hebrews 13:17—about church leaders. It says they have to actively watch out for the souls of those they lead because they'll have to give an account to the Lord one day for their leadership and oversight. It made me realize that it's true for the leader of any organization—especially for a husband who has to watch out for his wife and kids. Is this making sense, or am I overstepping my bounds?"

From the Word
What do you think? Does leadership extend to watching out for the moral and spiritual safety of those you lead?

According to Scripture, the answer is a definite "YES!" The elders referred to in Hebrews 13:7 and 17 were prepared to answer to God for the spiritual growth of those they led. God places leaders over others not only for the direction of their activities but for the care of their souls as well. There is a fine line here, of course. Genuine spiritual leadership does not mean heavy-handed control or undue invasion of privacy. Biblical leaders should demonstrate the same kind of balanced concern that God does.

For the Heart
This is a sensitive area for couples to discuss together. A wife who has been uncared for can feel unloved and insecure. A husband who has crossed the line from concern to control can find his wife resentful of his leadership efforts.

Each of you pick a number between 1 and 10 (1 = ineffective, 10 = very effective) that represents your perception of the husband's spiritual oversight of the wife. Is it gentle and loving, but clearly evident? Compare your numbers, identify your differences, and work together to close the gap—at a 10+!

A husband's "soul" job is not his sole job—but close to it!

DEVOTIONAL 2

Leading by the Book

SCRIPTURE
Ephesians 5:23a

For the husband is head of the wife, as also Christ is head of the church.

Betty's tears made silent paths down her cheeks late on a dark winter afternoon. Her quiet sobs and far-off gaze were interrupted by Dwayne's All-American, high-energy entry—the man-child, home from college for the weekend.

"Mom! How's it going? Brought you a present!" he crowed, hoisting a dirty clothes bag high like a hunter-gatherer would a downed goose. "Whoa—Mom, what's the matter? Sorry—I didn't know you were, uh, feeling bad," offered Dwayne, catching sight of Betty's puffy eyes and glistening cheeks.

"It's okay—I'll explain later. Right now, I'm just glad you're home!" said Betty as she hugged the only man of her house.

Over supper, Betty unraveled the feelings that brought the tears: "I came home from work and tried to read this property tax notice that was in the mail. I didn't understand it, and got all frustrated, and then started thinking about how your father used to take care of these things. I still miss him being the head of our home—you know, the leader, the problem-solver. It just made me cry."

Dwayne struggled silently, trying to be counselor, friend, pastor, and son. Hurting for his wounded mother. Consciously trying to help; subconsciously asking for help.

"Uh, I understand, Mom. No problem. But really—what are you supposed to do? You chose not to remarry when Dad died. That's okay—but doesn't that mean you're the head of this home now?"

From the Word

Life is not always as tidy as we would like, and Scripture does not directly answer every question. But where the Bible is lacking in specifics, a guiding principle can always be found. In this case, the clear teaching of Ephesians 5:23 is that the man is the head of the wife and of their relationship. He is, therefore, head of their home. Should he be passive, absent, or even deceased, the wife is not promoted to "head of the home"—though she may have to perform some of those tasks. While Betty may have to assume some of her former husband's duties, her role is a temporal exception to the rule, not a rewriting of it. The difference may be subtle—but it is substantial.

For the Heart

What is the status of your marriage? Is the husband present or absent? If present, is he fulfilling his Biblical mandate to be the head of the wife and of his home?

Whether the husband is present or absent, passive or active, has the wife tried to assume the role of head of the marriage or home?

Bow for a brief moment of prayer and ask God to give you wisdom to apply His eternal principles regarding the husband's headship in your marriage. He knows your situation, and will answer your prayer with compassion.

Principles are often illuminated by the light of a rare exception.

DEVOTIONAL 3

What the World Needs

SCRIPTURE
Proverbs 31:10–31

Her husband is known in the gates, when he sits among the elders of the land. Her husband also, . . . praises her.
(verses 23, 28b)

"Mom!" Lillith exclaimed. "Look at your calendar! You *are* planning on slowing down one of these years, aren't you?"

Alice laughed with her daughter, "Maybe someday, dear. But you know your father and I never really believed much in retirement."

"Well, I certainly know what pod this pea came out of," Lillith said confidently, pointing to herself. "You and I are alike in a lot of ways, Mom. Busy, getting things done, making it happen, right?! The world needs more women like us, don't you think? . . . Mom? . . . Oh boy, what did I say?"

The sunny, cheerful Alice that everyone loved became the mom Lillith had seen frequently since her divorce from Larry: sober, concerned, burdened. Whatever she had said, Lillith was sorry it slipped out. The sun had been covered by a cloud.

"Lillith, I don't disagree entirely. You and I are somewhat alike. But there is a big difference between what drives you and what drives me. I guess I could illustrate it best by saying that the world doesn't need more women like you and me as much as it needs more men like your father."

"What? Hello-o-o . . . It's not the Dark Ages, Mom, . . . Remember?"

"I remember all too well," said Alice. "Lillith—here, take this Bible—let me show you something . . ."

"Oh, Mom, please, not now . . ." groaned Lillith.

"Yes, now. When I get back from Vera's in a minute, I'll show you what I'm talking about—it's in Proverbs 31."

From the Word

Interestingly, Proverbs 31, most noted for its comments about the wife, also offers insight into the role of the husband.

In verses 23 and 28, the husband is pictured as engaged in the civic and professional duties of his day. His leadership style allowed for the full expression of his wife's many and varied talents. He was apparently not threatened by her successes. Rather, he encouraged her to fulfill her role as a wife—which she apparently did exceptionally! In fact, the text seems to imply that his being "known in the gates" was in no small part due to his wife. His leadership style was mutually beneficial!

For the Heart

How about the husband's leadership style in your marriage? Is it a style that encourages the wife to be all she can be within her God-given role?

Husbands, ask yourself whether any resistance to your leadership from your wife could be from stifling her God-given talents. Wives, are you content where God has placed you in your marriage—as the wife—as your husband's helper?

Husbands, identify one way you can more clearly define your role today that at the same time encourages your wife in hers.

Leadership that liberates—now that's a leadership STYLE!

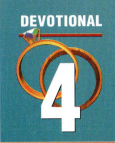

DEVOTIONAL 4

The Need to Lead

SCRIPTURE
1 Corinthians 9:16

For if I preach the gospel, I have nothing to boast of, for necessity is laid upon me; yes, woe is me if I do not preach the gospel!

Near noon on a typical Saturday, Deb was growing a bit frustrated with the answers she was getting from Bob. Her requests had been turned down twice already that morning.

Bob's schedule had been sort of —no, VERY— unreasonable lately, Deb was thinking. It showed on her face, and was about to in her voice.

"Why are you so busy?" Deb burst out. "Since when does working on the budget take priority over me?"

"What? Uh... What's that mean?" Bob asked, pushing back from his desk.

"Well, for the last several weekends, it seems like you've been glued to this desk. Every time I've needed something, you say you don't have time!"

"Well, you know, I guess you're right, Deb. Maybe I haven't explained myself very well. To be honest, I've been a little embarrassed to..."

"Embarrassed about what?" Deb asked—with a little less of an edge.

"Well, ever since Pastor Kallan preached about Paul's life not long ago—on the mandate he had from God to spread the Gospel? Remember?"

"I remember."

"It was like Paul actually feared not fulfilling the leadership role God had given him. You know, 'Woe is me' if I don't do this. Well, I got to thinking about my leading our family. How I've been putting off doing a budget, and getting our finances in shape. And I started thinking, 'Woe is me...!' I guess my need to lead went up a few notches after that sermon!"

From the Word

Amazing, isn't it? The Apostle Paul was so utterly convinced of his mandate from God—his "need to lead" among the churches—that he feared (in a healthy sense) not doing so! His fear of God drove him daily to fulfill what God had appointed him to do. Granted, Paul was an apostle—and we are not. But we are people in various leadership positions in life, all of which we should view like Paul viewed his: *I am here by God's appointment. Therefore, I need to fulfill His expectations. I need to lead in this area!* This should especially be true for a husband as he leads his wife.

God's expectations for husbands are as clear as they were for apostles. And since they are *God's* expectations, our task is clear!

For the Heart

Husbands, think about how you are fulfilling the leadership role in your marriage. Do you have that healthy sense of fear—what the Bible presents as a sort of "awesome respect"—for God's placement of you as leader in your marriage? And wives, are you comfortable with the demands made on leaders—the time that leadership tasks often require?

Husband, what is the area in which your wife has experienced insecurity or fear due to less-than-ideal leadership? Can you purpose to bless her anew today—by leading in a practical way in that area?

Don't let "Slow is me" become "Woe is me" in your future!

DEVOTIONAL 5

The Power of a Picture

SCRIPTURE
John 13:15

"For I have given you an example, that you should do as I have done to you."

Bob was concerned—maybe more like frustrated, moving toward angry. Sitting in Pastor Kallan's office, he struggled for the right words to describe his feelings.

"I don't know what's wrong, Jim. No matter what I say to Deb, it seems like I can't get through to her on this. I've tried all the approaches I know. I've said it gently, firmly, creatively, humorously—you name it. I don't know if she's choosing not to respond, or just doesn't care about people!"

"Bob, maybe the problem is not the words you're using, but your own actions. Let me ask you—when was the last time you reached out to a non-Christian neighbor yourself to welcome them to the neighborhood, or help them on a Saturday?"

"Me? Oh, I guess I can't remember. But that's really Deb's job—I mean, she's home all day, and could be having a real impact for Christ on our neighbors. I've asked her to make this a priority, but—well, I've already told you her response."

"Bob, I know Deb, and I know she's not an uncaring neighbor or a rebellious wife. I think she's struggling with your example!

"You know from your own management experience that people resent being asked to do things that their leaders aren't willing to do, right? Makes them feel used. Here's my idea: No more talk! Instead, why don't you start reaching out to your neighbors. Let's see if your example has a greater impact on Deb than your words have. It couldn't have any less, could it?"

From the Word

Jesus Christ was not the first person to use an example as a teaching method. His example of washing the disciples' feet, though, is probably the most famous in the world! Could Christ have delivered a lecture, or even told a parable about service—its cost, the humility it requires, its effect on the one served? Of course, and He did speak words to that effect in the Upper Room, but only after He had served them by washing their feet! His words probably took on a whole new meaning to the disciples after they saw Him demonstrate how to serve. This is another example of what made Christ the world's greatest leader.

For the Heart

Husbands, is there a "sore spot" between you and your wife that is not going away? Something you have asked her to do that she seems resistant or hesitant toward?

While a failure to lead by example is certainly not the cause in every case, it is definitely worth a second look! Stop and think of any areas of your marriage in which your expectations for your wife are higher than your own personal practice. If asking forgiveness is in order—to God or your wife—do so today.

Then—no more talk! Live out what you expect others to do!

Pictures are worth 1,000 words, but actions are worth 1,000,000!

LOVING:
The Responsibility of the Husband

All of a husband's responsibilities in marriage can be summarized in one Biblical command: Love your wife! And all of a husband's expressions of love can be illustrated in one Biblical example: As Christ loved the church. ■

CLASS NOTES

LOVING:
The Responsibility of the Husband

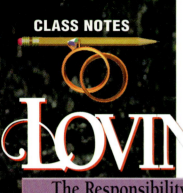

INTRODUCTION

_____
_____
_____
_____

 What is the nature of the love a husband should have for his wife (Ephesians 5:25)?

1. The husband is to love as _____ loved.

2. The husband's love for his wife is an _____ command.

3. The husband is to love his wife by his _____ and in his _____.

4. The husband is to keep on actively _____ to love his wife.

_____
_____
_____
_____
_____

hat are the three ways a husband is to love his wife?

1. Love your wife with _____ love, as Christ loved the church (Ephesians 5:25).

2. Love your wife as you love your own _____ (Ephesians 5:28–29).

3. Love your wife as you love _____ (Ephesians 5:33).

_____
_____
_____
_____

CONCLUSION

_____
_____
_____
_____
_____
_____
_____

EVALUATION

Loving:
The Responsibility of the Husband

Love. Easy to say, but much more challenging to demonstrate. Fortunately, Scripture provides a model for husbands—Jesus Christ and His love for the church.

How well is the husband demonstrating love to the wife in your marriage? Does the wife feel loved?

If you and your spouse score this evaluation differently, don't worry! Use this tool to explore the similarities and differences in each of your perceptions of giving and receiving love.

How is the husband fulfilling his responsibility to love his wife? Total your score below.

		False		Sometimes				True
A	The wife feels unconditionally loved and accepted by her husband.	1	2	3	4	5	6	7
B	The husband chooses to act and react lovingly even when he does not "feel" the emotion of love at the time.	1	2	3	4	5	6	7
C	The husband expresses love to his wife in ways that are particularly meaningful to her.	1	2	3	4	5	6	7
D	The husband demonstrates patience and gentleness rather than frustration and anger.	1	2	3	4	5	6	7
E	The husband portrays his wife to others in a positive, gracious light.	1	2	3	4	5	6	7
F	The husband is a good listener and "sounding board" for his wife.	1	2	3	4	5	6	7
G	The husband places his wife's personal needs above his own.	1	2	3	4	5	6	7
H	The husband helps his wife succeed in her roles and responsibilities within the marriage.	1	2	3	4	5	6	7

Column Subtotals:

The Husband's "Loving" Score
- **48–56** On Valentine's Day, gives a personalized gift.
- **38–47** On Valentine's Day, gives flowers and candy.
- **28–37** On Valentine's Day, sends warmest regards.
- **18–27** On Valentine's Day, sends card "postage due."
- **8–17** On Valentine's Day, experiences amnesia!

GRAND TOTAL:

1 What are the primary influences in today's society that encourage husbands and wives to love themselves more than each other?

2 How does Scripture define a husband's love for his wife? What might a wife do that would hinder her husband from loving her in this way?

3 How do family backgrounds impact the ways in which husbands and wives express love to each other and receive love from each other? How can such differences be overcome?

4 How would the average husband say he proves his love to his wife? What would the typical wife say truly makes her feel loved by her husband?

5 Can you think of a time in your parents' marriage when your father proved his love for your mother in a significant way? What impact does tender, nourishing love have on a wife?

PROJECT: DECIDE TO LOVE

Reflect on what you appreciate about your spouse for at least ten minutes. To get started, **list** unique personality traits, talents and skills (athletic, intellectual, social, decorative, etc.), character qualities, beliefs and convictions, accomplishments (both personal and professional), and the growth and positive changes you have observed over the years. **Add** to your list each day for a week. Once you have been reminded of all the things you love and appreciate about your mate, go on to the next logical step; **select** how you will express your love to your spouse in some creative way next week.

INTERACTION

On the Lighter Side

"He that falls in love with himself will have no rivals."
 —Benjamin Franklin

"Marriage requires falling in love many times—always with the same person."

"Marriage is too often a process whereby love ripens into vengeance."

BIBLE STUDY

LOVING

Easy Come, Easy Go

During courtship and early marriage, expressing love is relatively easy. As time goes by, however, demonstrating true love may become a bit more challenging. It is not uncommon to hear from someone considering divorce, "But we just don't love each other anymore."

That may even be true in your marriage, but the situation is not hopeless. Christ-like love *can* be nurtured in your marriage. Discover the joy of obedience as you allow God's Word to impact you . . . and your marriage.

1. Love's Commitment
Ephesians 5:25–29

How is the husband to love his wife?

What does it mean for a husband to "nourish" and "cherish" his wife?

In your marriage, how does the wife respond when she is nourished and cherished by her husband?

In what two ways could the husband nourish and cherish the wife that would make the greatest difference in your marriage?

2. Love's Contrast
Proverbs 15:17

What attitude can bring great unhappiness to a home even when there is an abundance of material possessions?

What are some of the ways that hatred can manifest itself in a marriage?

Identify a time in your marriage when an unloving attitude brought great unhappiness.

In your marriage, what does the husband do or say that makes the wife feel unloved the most?

What have you observed to be the consequences of unkind comments or actions by the husband toward the wife?

6.6   A BIBLICAL PORTRAIT OF MARRIAGE

© 1995 by Dr. Bruce H. Wilkinson and Walk Thru the Bible Ministries, Inc. Do not reproduce.

3. Love's Choice
Genesis 24:67

What is stated in this verse about Isaac's relationship to Rebekah?

What emotions does a wife feel when she knows her husband has chosen to love *her*?

What are some of the things the wife does in your marriage that make it difficult for the husband to express love to her?

In your marriage, what is the most important thing the husband could choose to do to cause the wife to feel loved?

4. Love's Praise
Proverbs 31:28–29

In this passage, how does the husband express his love?

What impact can genuine praise have on a wife?

List three characteristics of your spouse that are praiseworthy.

Describe how you will express praise to your spouse today.

5. Love's Sacrifice
Genesis 29:18–20

How did Jacob demonstrate the depth of his love for Rachel?

In your marriage, describe a time when the husband demonstrated sacrificial love for the wife.

How does the wife wish the husband would be more sacrificial right now in your marriage?

Husband, will you commit (or recommit) yourself to love your wife as God has commanded? Wife, will you do what you can to be easy to love? Demonstrate your commitment by initialing and dating this page.

Your initials and date

Loving: The Responsibility of the Husband

A Man's Mission in Marriage

DEVOTIONAL 1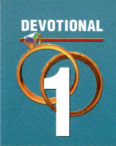

SCRIPTURE: Ephesians 5:25–33

> Husbands, love your wives, just as Christ also loved the church and gave Himself for it. (verse 25)

Into the garage roared "The Man On a Mission." Home from work, and disguised as a file cabinet, Bob, Jr., spilled into the kitchen with enough briefcases, notebooks, and commotion to start a new federal agency.

Kicking the door shut, he turned around and faced them—Deb and the kids, frozen in their tracks, not sure whether to hug or hide.

"Got a HUGE presentation tomorrow at work. Bosses from headquarters are here. Got to go study this stuff and get a report ready. I'll eat later."

He failed to notice Deb's bathrobe, her pale face, puffy eyes, and haggard look. She had gone downhill rapidly all afternoon with fever and chills competing for control of her body. And the nausea! She could hardly stand up.

About 10:30 that night, Kim appeared in the living room—now "The War Room."

"Uh, Dad, I think you better come see about Mom. She's in the bathroom moaning and groaning—I think she's about to throw up. Did you know she's been feeling sick all afternoon?"

Bob stopped his work and looked up at Kim: "She has? Okay, honey. I'll be right there."

She didn't look sick to me, Bob thought as he realized he didn't remember what she looked like when he came in earlier.

Heading upstairs, his conscience was troubled by the thoughts he was having. *Why tonight? I don't have time to be a nurse. My entire career could be ruined if I blow this presentation tomorrow.*

From the Word

It is not surprising that Bob's conscience was troubled. Not surprising, that is, in light of Scriptures like Ephesians 5:25.

As unrealistic as it may seem, Scripture establishes the love of Christ for the church as the example for a husband to follow in loving his wife. What does it mean to love one's wife as Christ loved the church? Sacrificially, consistently, by choice—all of that, at least. More specifically, it means when it is not convenient, when you would rather be doing something else, and especially when it might keep you from meeting your agenda! That was Bob's situation, and he—his heart, that is—knew it!

For the Heart

All husbands at times resent the intrusion of their wife's needs. But all husbands can—and should—learn to love as Christ loved.

Husband, is there a spot on your conscience which is a shade of grey instead of pure white? An area where your love for your wife has been less than Christ's love? You can clean that spot today by setting aside your agenda and your wants and focusing on your wife's needs. Will you do so?

Wife, have you resented not being loved perfectly? Clear your conscience as well and, in doing so, become an even purer bride!

When a man loves his wife sacrificially, he loves like Christ.

DEVOTIONAL 2

The Meaning of Honor

SCRIPTURE
1 Peter 3:7–12

Likewise you husbands, dwell with them with understanding, giving honor to the wife, as to the weaker vessel, and as being heirs together of the grace of life, that your prayers may not be hindered.

(verse 7)

It didn't seem to Bob, Sr., that life could look a whole lot better than it did that Saturday. The crisp, fall morning seemed to be telling Bob he was "King for a Day." He loved it.

Mentally, he was already planning his agenda:

First, he'd catch his two favorite Saturday morning fishing shows on television, then do his daily Bible study, then maybe spin over to a couple of sports stores and bait shops just to make sure nothing new had come in since his last visit—two days before.

"Honey . . . oh, h-o-n-e-y. Earth to Bob." It was Alice, gently interrupting the "King." He didn't mind—her sweet demeanor was never an interruption. Well, rarely ever. Why did he feel an exception to the rule coming?

"I have to drive a couple of seniors from the nursing home over to the outlet mall in Blairsville, Bob. They called last night, and I just couldn't say 'No.' I was wondering if you'd drive us over since you're free today?"

The "King" refocused out the window. His perfect Saturday kingdom had vanished! Crisp was now crummy. Fishing had become wishing. The hammock became a shopping cart, and his specialty smoked ribs . . . a limp mallburger. He decided to stand his ground—it's what kings do.

"Alice, I'm sorry. I have a number of things I had planned to do today. The nursing home is your ministry, and you'll just have to drive them yourself." With that he excused himself and went to the den—his fishing shows were starting.

From the Word

The "King for a Day's" crown is looking a little tarnished, wouldn't you agree? Perhaps you have experienced this in your marriage: The wife has a practical need, the importance of which the husband just does not understand. A sure recipe for conflict.

When the Apostle Peter addressed this issue in one of his letters, he insisted that husbands live with their wives in ways that communicate and show understanding. What does understanding say to a wife? It says, "Honor." It says, "I honor you by appreciating your idea, your request, and your desire. Though it is not the same as I would do, I will honor you by helping fulfill your desire to the best of my ability." To this, Peter would probably say a hearty, "Amen!"

For the Heart

When was the last time in your marriage that the husband had an opportunity to honor the wife by showing understanding—but failed to do so?

Husband, would you mention that "missed opportunity" to your wife today and seek her forgiveness? And, purpose to begin demonstrating understanding—by faith, if necessary! What seems like a small (and perhaps to a husband insignificant) gesture can crush, or blossom, the spirit of a wife.

Wife, acknowledge your husband's efforts to show you honor!

How do you spell "honor your wife?" U-N-D-E-R-S-T-A-N-D-I-N-G.

Loving: The Responsibility of the Husband 6.9

DEVOTIONAL 3

When the Loving Gets Tough

SCRIPTURE
Romans 5:6–11

But God demonstrates His own love toward us, in that while we were still sinners, Christ died for us.

(verse 8)

Dwayne was getting in his car at Bob and Deb's when his uncle pulled in the driveway behind him.

"Uncle Bob," Dwayne called. "How 'ya doing?"

"Great, Dwayne. What brings you over?"

"Just dropping off some of my outgrown clothes for Bobby. Mom and Aunt Deb thought he could wear some of 'em."

"Great! Thanks for bringing them over. Hey—how's school going? Making all A's, I presume. And—I've been meaning to ask you, big guy—how's the old love life? You and Sherry getting ready for the big day?"

Before Dwayne could answer, Bob knew he had hit a nerve. The downcast eyes, shuffling feet, and hemming and hawing were all symptoms of the this-is-worse-than-a-root-canal syndrome.

"What's wrong, Dwayne?" Bob asked. "Everything okay? Can I help with anything?"

"Well, you can explain women to me for starters," Dwayne blurted out. "I mean, I know Sherry's the right girl to marry, and all, and, yes, we're getting along fine. But man—she and I had a disagreement at school this week that I couldn't believe! That's why I'm home this weekend. I had to get away and think this through. She did something that I thought was just plain uncalled-for. I didn't think people who love you would treat you that way."

"I hear you, pal. Gets rough sometimes, doesn't it?"

"Yeah. This business of love is tougher than I thought!"

From the Word

Welcome to the real world, Dwayne! The idea that people never act inappropriately in serious relationships is a misconception. Just as moving from one country to another doesn't change your name, so moving from single to married doesn't change your nature. It remains sinful, through and through!

Scripture shows how Christ's love for the church is a model of how husbands are to love their wives: even if they act like a sinner (see Romans 5:8). And while sin in marriage is a two-way street, Scripture puts upon the man the task of loving with Christ-like love—in the same way Christ loved the man though he was a sinner.

For the Heart

Husband, think of the time when you were the most hurt by something your wife said or did. Hurt means beyond mad. It's the "How could she have done this to me?" type of discouragement. It's the "How can we have a relationship after this?" kind of feeling.

Have you truly forgiven (loved) your wife in spite of this event? Not sure? Would you bow your head right now and tell Christ that you will love your wife like He loves you—as a sinner? If your wife is unsure of your love, tell her as well.

And wives—get ready to be loved.

When the loving gets tough, the tough get loving.

DEVOTIONAL 4

The Right Kind of Fear

SCRIPTURE
Psalm 128:1–3

Blessed is every one who fears the Lord … Your wife shall be like a fruitful vine in the very heart of your house.

(verses 1, 3a)

"Okay, Granddad—thanks again. I'll see you Saturday." Dwayne hung up the phone in his dorm room. His grandfather's grape arbor would be the perfect focus for his botany paper—and the lab would begin bright and early Saturday.

It was early fall, harvest time, and the grapevines were bowing under the weight of the bunches. "Wow, Granddad! Look at the grapes," Dwayne exclaimed as they entered the arbor. "Unbelievable. How do you do it? My botany professor would be impressed!"

"Well, first you have to retire, Dwayne, so you can baby these things along, oh, eight to ten hours every day," laughed his grandfather. After an hour of making notes and taking pictures, Bob's voice became soft. "See this vine, Dwayne. It's the most fruitful one I have. I've named it 'Alice'—after you-know-who."

"Grandmother Alice?" Dwayne asked. "Why?"

"Because it's so fruitful. It bears so much fruit, so consistently, year after year. It just reminds me of your grandmother that way. I don't know another Christian lady who lives a more fruitful life than your Grandmother Alice.

"Dwayne, when your grandmother and I were first married, an old farmer I knew then—he owned a vineyard, too—gave me a Bible verse to build my marriage and my home on. He said it had worked for him, and it would work for me. And it has."

"Really? Wait a minute—let me write this down."

From the Word

What verse would you give a young man to ensure that his wife would be like a fruitful vine in their home? If you recommended Psalm 128, you would do him a great favor.

This passage says that a man's wife will be like a fruitful vine in the very heart of their home if he will do one thing: Fear the Lord. And what is "fearing the Lord"? It is that enduring perspective of God—and one's relationship with Him—that results in awe, in worship, and in obedience to His commands. A husband who fears the Lord will have a wife who bears fruit for the Lord. But be careful! Husbands should fear the Lord because He is God, not to get a fruitful wife. The former serves God, the latter serves self.

For the Heart

Husband, it is time to take a closer look at your perspective of God—and your relationship with Him. How much do you fear Him? That is, how much awe, how much worship, and how much obedience to His commands can be found in your life?

Do you believe any lack of fruit in your wife's life could be tied to a lack of your fearing the Lord?

Use this moment to search your heart, and make things right with Him.

Wife, how much fruit is there in your spiritual life? Remember, a husband's lack of fearing the Lord is no excuse for spiritual barrenness.

The fear of God in your life will put the fruit of God in your wife!

DEVOTIONAL 5

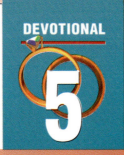

Back to the Basics

SCRIPTURE
1 Corinthians 13:1–13

And now abide faith, hope, love, these three; but the greatest of these is love.

(verse 13)

"Larry! I thought that was you!" Dan Burton called out, approaching Larry's booth. "Good to see you!"

Pastor Burton's towering presence was intimidating enough. But the fact that he had married Larry and Lillith, then tried to prevent their divorce, made their encounter somewhat awkward at first.

"Hello, Pastor. How are you?" Larry managed.

"Now tell me, Larry. How is it that two classy guys like us are forced to get our nourishment from a place like The Burger Mill?" Dan Burton was looking for an invitation to sit down.

"I don't know, just lucky I guess. Uh, would you like to sit down?" Larry said.

"Sure. Thanks. Don't mind if I do. I'm here by myself between meetings. So, how are you?"

"Oh, I'm doing okay… I guess. Still trying to figure out what went wrong with Lillith and me. I've never had a chance to thank you for all you did to try to help us, Pastor. It meant a lot. Maybe we just weren't ready to hear what we needed to hear. Do you think that's possible?"

"Sure, it's possible. You and Lillith went through some deep water together. All of us probably have to learn some things the hard way. I know I have! You know, Larry, as I've reflected on your divorce from Lillith, and all of the things we talked about in counseling, it seems there was one key ingredient missing in your marriage." The pastor filled his mouth with a bite of his MillMeister Deluxe, leaving the ball in Larry's court.

"Are you kidding? There had to be more than one thing missing!"

From the Word

Scripture is very clear about what has the highest value in God's kingdom. Without question, it is love. God Himself is called "love," and Jesus commanded us to love God and our neighbor above all else. Surely this ethical priority holds true in marriage, the most important and intense of all human relationships. The Apostle Paul seemed to think so as he instructed the believers at Corinth. To paraphrase 1 Corinthians 13:13 in the language of husbands, "A husband can be spiritual, he can be optimistic, he can be loyal and kind—he can be lots of wonderful things—but above all, the greatest thing he can be toward his wife is loving." Without love, his actions are like sounding brass.

For the Heart

Husband, as we end this series of devotionals designed to encourage you to love your wife, take a quick inventory. Jot down the top five positive things you think you "are" to your wife, for example, provider, friend, or encourager. Does "lover" (and not just in the physical sense) rank #1? Is the greatest thing on your list "love"?

If not, can you make a commitment before God today to begin to love your wife in new and meaningful ways? (And wives, make a brief inventory of all the ways you can likewise love your husband!)

Loving husbands are easy to find. Just look for happy wives.

SESSION 7

IN-LAWS:
Ensure In-Laws Don't Become Out-Laws

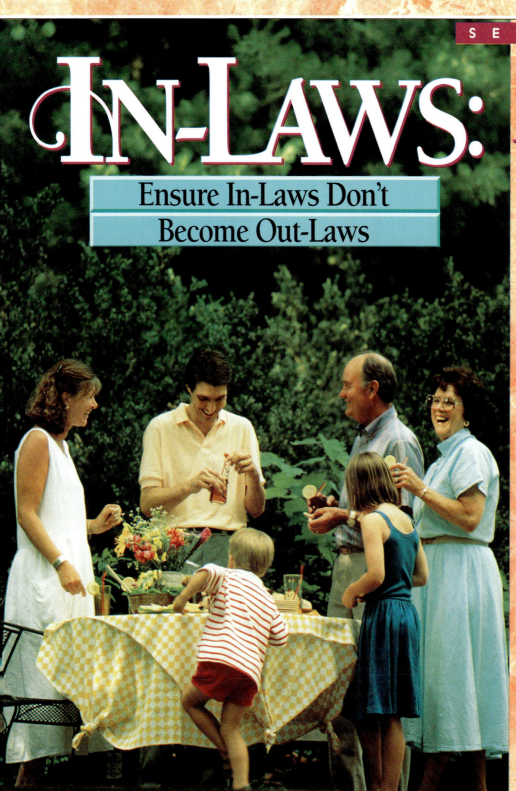

What emotion comes to mind when you hear the word "in-laws"? Discover how in-laws can become assets or liabilities when Biblical boundaries are either observed or ignored. ■

IN-LAWS:
Ensure In-Laws Don't Become Out-Laws

INTRODUCTION

_____

_____

_____

hat are the key instructions regarding marriage given in Genesis 2:24?

_____ and _____

n what Scripture passages is the child's responsibility to his or her parents presented?

_____   _____

_____   _____

_____

From these verses, how are children to respond to their parents?

_____ and _____

_____

_____

How do children and parents relate in the various seasons of marriage?

Stage One: Before Marriage _____

Stage Two: Early Marriage _____

Stage Three: Middle Marriage _____

Stage Four: Older Marriage _____

_____ _____

What are the five primary issues that must be dealt with in order for in-laws not to become "out-laws"?

1. _____   4. _____

2. _____   5. _____

3. _____

CONCLUSION

_____

_____

_____

_____

EVALUATION

In-Laws: Ensure In-Laws Don't Become Out-Laws!

How is your relationship with your parents? How about with your in-laws? This evaluation should reveal whether you are experiencing healthy or unhealthy relationships with these family members.

Try to evaluate the relationships you as a couple have with your in-laws. These issues may be emotional, but be willing to take whatever steps are necessary to strengthen your marriage. And do what you can to bring your relationships with both sets of parents to a new level of health and Biblical maturity.

Evaluate how you as a couple presently relate to both sets of parents. Total your score below.

		False			Sometimes			True
A	We show honor and respect to our parents, even when we may not feel they deserve it.	1	2	3	4	5	6	7
B	We have learned to ask for wise counsel from our parents, but are free to exercise our own judgment in the actual decisions.	1	2	3	4	5	6	7
C	Neither of us deliberately tears down our parents or in-laws to our spouse.	1	2	3	4	5	6	7
D	We are independent of our parents' control and authority. We don't feel obligated to obey their every wish.	1	2	3	4	5	6	7
E	We respectfully yet firmly choose which activities will be done with (or without) the in-laws.	1	2	3	4	5	6	7
F	We both accept the humanity of our parents and have chosen to forgive them for any wrongs done against us.	1	2	3	4	5	6	7
G	We are united, not taking sides with our parents against each other.	1	2	3	4	5	6	7
H	We enjoy a healthy, mature relationship with both sets of parents.	1	2	3	4	5	6	7

The Couple's "In-Laws" Score
- **48–56** "I love my in-laws!"
- **38–47** "Ask me about my in-laws."
- **28–37** "My in-laws? Short visits are OK."
- **18–27** "You don't know *my* in-laws!"
- **8–17** "Take my in-laws, PLEASE!"

Column Subtotals:

GRAND TOTAL:

INTERACTION

1. What are some of the most common sources of conflict between a couple and their in-laws? Why are these conflicts often more emotional than most?

2. What does the Biblical command "to honor" mean? What are some ways adult married children can show honor and respect for their parents?

3. What are some ways couples exclude their parents from their lives in a hurtful and disrespectful manner?

4. How does a parent's continuing bossiness affect the married son or daughter? What is the emotional response of the spouse when this happens?

5. How could a husband or wife practically demonstrate loyalty to the spouse over his or her parents?

On the Lighter Side

"No man is really successful until his in-laws admit it."

"Mother love is dangerous when it becomes *smother* love."

"Another reason for unhappy marriages is that men can't fool their wives like they could fool their mothers."

PROJECT: ENSURE HEALTHY IN-LAW FRIENDSHIPS

Most healthy relationships are built on respect. Enhance your relationship with your own parents and your in-laws by **tangibly honoring** them. Creatively **choose** how you will express your love and appreciation—letter, framed picture, audio tape, scrapbook, videotape, or some other creative means. Even if there are hurts in the past, **focus** on those things which are positive—happy memories, admirable character qualities, enduring family traditions, values, hobbies or skills they passed on, good advice they gave, etc. **Present** your "Tribute" in a special way and discover the blessing you get from blessing others.

BIBLE STUDY

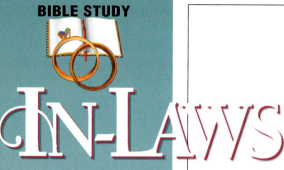

IN-LAWS

War or Peace?

Once you are married, your in-laws are part of your extended family for life. Yet all too often the relationship between a couple and their in-laws may resemble a battlefield. Fortunately, there are times when there is true friendship and peace between the couple and their parents.

Complete these Bible studies with a willingness to learn how to properly relate to your in-laws. Become a peacemaker and you will know God's peace, not war.

1. Paying Respect
Exodus 20:12

How are children to relate to their parents?

What does the word "honor" mean?

Since getting married, what are three common ways you show respect for your own parents?

In what one way will you demonstrate your honor for your parents within the next week? For your in-laws?

2. Being Human
Hebrews 12:9a

Who corrected us and to whom did we pay respect according to this passage?

Does this passage suggest that parents are only to be respected if they are worthy of respect?

What behavior or hurt do you need to forgive in order to freely show respect to your parents? To your in-laws?

What wrong should your spouse forgive in order to be able to freely demonstrate honor to his or her parents? To your parents?

7.6   A BIBLICAL PORTRAIT OF MARRIAGE

3. Giving Advice
Exodus 18:13–24

In verse 19, what did Jethro say he was going to give Moses?

What is the main difference between a "command" and "counsel"?

Describe a time when you received good counsel from your mother-in-law or father-in-law.

How do you tend to respond to unsolicited counsel from your in-laws?

The next time you receive advice from your in-laws that you really don't want, what could you respectfully say?

4. Causing Grief
Genesis 26:34–35

How did Esau's choice of wives affect Isaac and Rebekah, his parents?

What are some typical emotions parents might experience when they disagree with decisions that their adult children make?

In your marriage, what choice have you made that caused grief to your parents or your in-laws?

How specifically did your parents or in-laws respond to your decision?

Should your married children ever disappoint you greatly, how do you want to respond?

5. Showing Kindness
Ruth 1:6–14

Describe the relationship Naomi had with her daughters-in-law.

What are the benefits to a marriage when the relationship with the in-laws is harmonious and not strained?

What do you appreciate about your in-laws?

How do you "deal kindly" toward your in-laws?

What do you wish your spouse would do or say to show kindness to your parents?

Will you do everything you can to strengthen your own marriage while developing healthy, harmonious relationships with your parents and your in-laws? Demonstrate your commitment by initialing and dating this page.

Your initials and date

In-Laws: Ensure In-Laws Don't Become Out-Laws   7.7

DEVOTIONAL 1

Develop a Friend-in-Law

SCRIPTURE
Exodus 4:18

So Moses went and returned to Jethro his father-in-law, and said to him, "Please let me go and return to my brethren who are in Egypt, and see whether they are still alive." And Jethro said to Moses, "Go in peace."

Dwayne's hands were still locked on the steering wheel a full minute after he pulled up to Sherry's house. These visits with his future in-laws made him nervous.

After a great meal and lots of "let's-get-to-know-our-future-son-in-law" dinner conversation, Dwayne and Sherry's dad went into the den.

"Uh, Mr. Williams, I wanted to talk with you about something if you have a minute."

"A minute? Unless you're leaving, we've got all night. Go right ahead."

"Okay, uh, I . . . I just wanted to bring you up to date on the plans I've been considering for my future—I mean, Sherry's and my future—after we're married."

"Good, good. I've been looking forward to discussing this with you."

Uh-oh, Dwayne thought. *He's already got plans for me to go to work at his bank. I knew it! Oh man, why'd I bring this up?*

"Well, you know my major has been marine biology and I really believe after Sherry and I graduate that I'd like to go on to grad school to work on my masters and Sherry and I have talked it over and she's willing to support me in those plans and I believe we can make it financially and I think Sherry will be fine and . . ."

"Whoa, Dwayne. Whoa! Who are you trying to convince? Me or you? Listen: You need to know that Ann and I believe in you, and trust your choices. After all, you chose Sherry for a wife, right?" Mr. Williams winked. "You and Sherry are planning *your* lives, not ours—and you have our blessing!"

From the Word

Mr. Williams must have taken lessons from Jethro, the father-in-law of Moses. An instructive example of "in-lawing" is the one in Exodus chapters 4 and 18 showing the relationship between Moses and his father-in-law. (Our devotionals this week will center on their relationship.) In chapter 4, verse 18, Moses is instructed by God to leave the land of Midian with his family and return to Egypt to lead the Israelites out of bondage. When Moses decides to leave, Jethro (for whom Moses worked) speaks an ancient blessing upon him, "Go in peace." Or, "You have my permission, but more importantly, my blessing, to go your own way."

For the Heart

Normally, in-laws are more desirous of giving their blessing than their permission to their married children—but often don't have the chance to do either. Sometimes their voicing of an unsolicited opinion is a response to feeling "shut out" of their married children's lives.

Talk with your spouse about the current state of "communication" with your in-laws. Choose an area of your marriage or family where change is occurring and start communicating positively and openly with your in-laws about it. You may receive an unexpected blessing!

There ought to be a law about in-laws! There is. Commandment #5.

7.8 A BIBLICAL PORTRAIT OF MARRIAGE

© 1995 by Dr. Bruce H. Wilkinson and Walk Thru the Bible Ministries, Inc. Do not reproduce.

DEVOTIONAL 2

Careful What You Ask for!

SCRIPTURE
Exodus 18:13–26

So Moses heeded the voice of his father-in-law and did all that he had said.

(verse 24)

"Since you've asked me, Deb, I'll tell you. But can I ask you something else first?" Alice brought her coffee with her and sat down at the kitchen table across from Deb.

"Well, sure, . . ." Deb's voice was trailing off because she was surprised at her mother-in-law's response. *Alice is taking this a bit more seriously than I intended,* Deb thought.

"I just want to ask you how seriously you want my advice—before I give it! Here's why. You've asked me a pretty serious question. You want advice about your own daughter—my granddaughter. Because Kim is my granddaughter, I have strong feelings about her—you know, what's best for her. Do you understand?"

"Yes, I'm just not sure what it all means. But go on."

"Well, let's say I give you some advice that you don't agree with, and so you don't take it. You do what you want to do instead of what I suggest. Will you have the courage and the freedom to do that? Or will you feel obligated to do what I suggest because I'm Kim's grandmother—and your mother-in-law?"

"Hmmm. I see what you mean. I could get stuck in a difficult position, and so it might be safer not even to ask?"

"That's right. Kim is your daughter first, my granddaughter a distant second. If you ask for my advice, you have to treat it as exactly what it is: An opinion. That's all. So—do you still want my advice?"

Deb took a deep breath, like she was on a TV quiz show about to risk it all to go for the grand prize. "Okay! I'm ready to hear it, Alice. And thanks."

From the Word

Wow! How's that for a wise mother-in-law? How often do in-laws give their opinions without thinking of the consequences? The old "why'd you ask if you weren't going to do it?" response is always lurking behind "unheeded" advice.

When Moses was faced with the enormously difficult task of judging the problems of the nation of Israel, his father-in-law, Jethro, came with some advice. Scripture is clear that Jethro offered "counsel," not a command, to his son-in-law. In fact, he concludes his advice with a qualifier: Do this only if God commands you (verse 23). As it turned out, Moses successfully applied the advice of his father-in-law. But be prepared—the results and advice can go either way!

For the Heart

First question: If you had been in Deb's shoes, what would you have done? Do you and your in-laws have an honest, open relationship? Could you set the example next time you need to give, or ask for, advice?

Secondly, has there been a time in your marriage when advice from an in-law was received, but not applied? Or was the advice applied but with unsuccessful results? Hurt feelings, lasting for years, have been known to start in situations like these!

If there is any healing that needs to take place over a sensitive "advice" situation, purpose to start the process.

**Ask, and you shall receive.
Therefore, be careful who you ask.**

DEVOTIONAL 3

How Could They Do That?

SCRIPTURE: Exodus 18:7

So Moses went out to meet his father-in-law, bowed down, and kissed him. And they asked each other about their well-being, and they went into the tent.

"You've got to call her, Bob. The sooner you get it over with, the better you'll feel." Deb was right, and Bob knew it.

He also knew that his mother-in-law was going to be very disappointed when she heard Bob's news: He and Deb and the kids were going to skip the annual 4th of July weekend at the beach with Deb's parents. The kids' schedules were conflicting, and it just wasn't going to work. Bob was dreading this call.

He dialed the number. "Too bad. Guess they're not home," Bob said as he prepared to hang up after only two rings.

"B-o-b, . . ." Deb smiled.

Deb's mother finally answered the phone—out of breath: "I'm sorry, Bob. I was in the garage looking for things for the weekend at the beach. And Dave—he's already got his fishing gear packed! He can't wait! Now, what was it you wanted, dear?"

By the end of the conversation, both felt awful: Bob, for standing his ground; Dorothy, for being "rejected" by her daughter and son-in-law.

"How could Bob and Deb do that?" Dorothy asked her husband. "This is an important family event—has been for years. Everyone will be there but them. It seems a bit thoughtless that they couldn't plan ahead, work out the kids' schedules, and be there!"

"Honey," Dave began, "could I ask a question? When you said that the weekend 'is an important family event,' whose family—singular—did you mean? Ours . . . or theirs? We are two separate families . . . Remember?"

From the Word

Parents often struggle with acknowledging that their grown children, when married, constitute separate households—with separate agendas and schedules—which need to be respected.

When Moses and his father-in-law, Jethro, met after an extended separation, note their mutual respect and affection for one another. In Exodus 18:7, it appears that there was no friction or tension between them. How did they manage their relationship? Apparently with a healthy dose of mutual respect! They were not only in-laws, but friends and "coworkers"—though with different schedules. They seemed to relate just the way in-laws should.

For the Heart

The longer you and your spouse are married, the clearer the roles and expectations should be between you and both sets of parents.

Is there tension caused by unclear expectations between all involved? Perhaps you and your spouse have differing perspectives on the nature of your relationship to your in-laws.

Have you had a situation like Bob and Deb's recently? If it didn't go well, discuss together how you as a couple can relate more effectively with your in-laws. If needed, talk directly with your in-laws as well.

Careful! All family schedules and priorities are not created equal.

DEVOTIONAL 4

Becoming Deeper-in-Laws

SCRIPTURE
Exodus 18:8–12

And Moses told his father-in-law all that the Lord had done to Pharaoh and to the Egyptians for Israel's sake, all the hardship that had come upon them on the way, and how the Lord had delivered them.

(verse 8)

"Betty, we were crazy about you when Will was alive, and we still are! You and Dwayne will always be family to us. I'm just sorry we don't get down to see you both more often."

Betty's "father-in-law" was as gentle and soothing as they come. One of the things that had endeared Betty to Will before they married was Will's parents. She couldn't imagine a more perfect pair of in-laws. And they had remained faithful, even after Will's death, to keep an eye on Betty and Dwayne in a variety of ways.

"So tell me, how's everything?" Wilson continued. "I want to know it all—the grit and the glory—no holds barred. You and Dwayne doing okay?"

Betty knew he meant it. Wilson was a bottom-line kind of guy who left no stones unturned in his thorough approach to relationships. Betty loved him for it, too—it felt good to have a wise man care about her life in a genuine and uplifting way.

After an hour or so of discussing Dwayne, his engagement, her own job and personal ups and downs, Betty was still on the surface. She sensed Wilson looking for more stones to turn.

"Now Betty, I need to ask you how your finances are holding up. I know your dad gives you advice in that area, and I'm not trying to interfere, but Kathy and I still want to make sure that you and Dwayne are doing okay? You know what I mean?"

"Yes, and I don't mind you asking, Wilson. I'd love your advice on a change I made in the money I've invested to see if you think it's wise."

From the Word

Maybe Wilson is the mold from which great fathers-in-law are made. Or maybe Jethro, Moses' father-in-law, was the mold. He certainly is presented that way in Scripture. In Exodus 18:8–12, Jethro and Moses sat and talked—just talked—apparently for hours. Moses recounted for Jethro the story of how God delivered Israel from Pharaoh in Egypt. What were they doing? *Communicating. Sharing important life experiences. Going deeper into one another's lives.* It's what all in-laws should do. This level of communication is Biblical and therefore emotionally healthy for all adults—but especially for those in extended families. Where distance separates, communication reunites.

For the Heart

When was the last time you had an extended time of conversation with one of your in-laws? No opinions, no critiques, no complaints. Just open, honest talk.

If you are the "parent-in-law," inquire about those things that you know are most important to your "child-in-law." Some issues lurk beneath the surface and need to be verbalized. Be open—they may even need to discuss *you*! And that's okay.

"Child-in-law," be sensitive to your in-laws' needs, their fears, and their future as they grow older. They need to know you care about them!

The quickest way to another's heart is to open up your own.

DEVOTIONAL 5

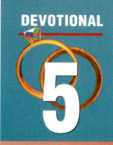

Extended Family: A Great Idea!

SCRIPTURE
Exodus 18:1–6, 27

Then Moses let his father-in-law depart, and he went his way to his own land.

(verse 27)

"Hey, kids. Dorothy and I just had a terrific idea! Wait'll you hear it! We're thinking we'll just sell our house, move cross-country, and set up shop right there near you folks—maybe the same subdivision! Is that a great idea or what? Don't you love it? Hello? Hello? You kids on the line there?"

"Uh, yes Dad, we're still here," Deb managed to reply. "Uh, that's uh, some idea! Yeah, wow, well, you kind of caught us by surprise. Yes, uh, that's a wonderful idea. Isn't it Bob?" Deb stuttered, hoping Bob hadn't hung up the other phone—which he had.

"I think Bob had to get off the phone a second, Dad. But I'm sure he'd think it was a great idea, too."

"Sure he will. Well, listen, you kids stay near the phone and we'll keep you posted on the details. We're calling the realtor tomorrow to get the house on the market! Deb, I've had some great ideas before, but this is probably the best, don't you think?"

"Well, it's some idea, Dad, you're right there. Well, thanks for calling, and keep us posted . . . Bye!"

Deb hung up the phone and turned around to find Bob leaning against the doorjamb. Arms folded, he had a "my-way-or-the-highway" look on his face.

"Was that a serious call, or a practical joke, Deb?"

"Serious, I think. Wow! Do you think they'd really do it?"

"Probably. But I've got an idea. Let's just swap houses with them. They want to move here? Fine. They can have our house and we'll take theirs."

From the Word

While Scripture doesn't speak specifically about how close married children and their in-laws should live, there are principles which offer guidance. For instance, in the case of Moses and his father-in-law, Jethro, Scripture clearly points out that Jethro came to see Moses for a purpose. When his purpose was completed, he went back to *his* home: ". . . and he went his way to his own land" (Exodus 18:1–6, 27). While not a command of Scripture, this passage illustrates how in-laws and their children usually have separate homes. On the other hand, there are exceptions to every rule, and in-laws can live close by with healthy results. Whether near or far, make it healthy!

For the Heart

Perhaps you and your spouse are in-laws already. If so, what has been your posture concerning the geographical distance between you and your married child(ren)?

Do all agree that your current status is the best one? Since people, not places, are the obvious main concern, can you identify what the relational issues are which have made your present status either ideal or less than ideal? Discuss these matters with your spouse. Do you both agree?

Stop and pray for your in-laws for a moment. Thank God *for* them—and for a bright future *with* them!

Extended families are kept close by extended hearts and hands.

SESSION 8

MONEY:
Control Money Through Covetousness or Contentment

*T*he *lack* of money is often blamed for many arguments in marriage, but the *love* of money is usually the real culprit. When the discipline of contentment is learned, money problems can be brought under control. ■

MONEY

Control Money Through Covetousness or Contentment

INTRODUCTION

he key passage on money in the Bible is _____:

Let your conduct be _____

_____, and be _____

with such things as you have.

hat are the results of a love of money taking root in one's life (1 Timothy 6:10)?

- Stray from the _____
- Pierce oneself with _____

Rather than finding your security from hoarding money or seeking pleasure from spending money, how *should* a person respond (Luke 12:13–31; 1 Timothy 6:17, 19; Hebrews 13:5–6)?

- Trust _____ rather than _____.
- _____ what you have with others.
- _____ your riches in heaven.
- Believe that God will _____ leave you nor forsake you.

_____

_____

What characterizes true contentment (1 Timothy 6:6–9)?

- Be content with _____ _____ _____.
- Be content with _____ and _____.

CONCLUSION

_____

_____

_____

_____

EVALUATION

**Money:
Control Money
Through Covetousness
or Contentment**

Is money a source of conflict in your marriage? This evaluation should help pinpoint the root issues that, if conquered, can bring peace to your lives.

You and your spouse may view money and money problems in very diverse ways. Use this quiz to stimulate open discussion of the financial issues that stir emotion and can bring conflict to your marriage relationship.

Couples, how well do you control money in your marriage? Total your score below.

		False		Sometimes			True
A	Success for us is determined by how we *use* the money we have, not by *how much* money we have.	1	2	3	4	5	6	7
B	We have very few arguments about money in our marriage.	1	2	3	4	5	6	7
C	We are not worried or fearful for the future, because our trust is in God rather than in accumulating money.	1	2	3	4	5	6	7
D	We regularly give to the Lord's work as part of our plan for money management.	1	2	3	4	5	6	7
E	We are not controlled either by a love of money or a love of things.	1	2	3	4	5	6	7
F	We are not wasteful or careless in spending the money we have.	1	2	3	4	5	6	7
G	We do not spend more money than we earn.	1	2	3	4	5	6	7
H	We are satisfied with what we have and are content with God's provision.	1	2	3	4	5	6	7

Column Subtotals:

The Couple's "Money" Score
- **48–56** Manages money with an open hand.
- **38–47** Has a good handle on the finances.
- **28–37** Tries to get a grip on the finances.
- **18–27** Has lost control of the finances.
- **8–17** "Keep your hands off my money!"

GRAND TOTAL:

A BIBLICAL PORTRAIT OF MARRIAGE

© 1995 by Dr. Bruce H. Wilkinson and Walk Thru the Bible Ministries, Inc. Do not reprod

1 What are some of the reasons people give for trying to get as much money as they can? What are the differences between saving and hoarding?

2 What impact does covetousness have on a person's relationship with others and with the Lord?

3 How does society encourage people to focus on spending money? What things or activities are considered "necessities" by today's standards?

4 What effect does debt have on a couple's emotions? What are the relational consequences of indebtedness?

5 What have you observed to be true of couples who seem to be experiencing financial contentment in their lives? How is contentment learned?

PROJECT: LEARN TO BE CONTENT

On a 3x5 index card, **write** the words "Be Content with What You Have" in bold letters. **Carry** this card with you for one week in a pocket, wallet, or planning calendar. As you contemplate financial decisions throughout the week, **stop and read** the card. **Evaluate** each purchasing decision in light of this principle. Do I really need this? Why do I want it? Will this put us in (or further in) debt? Can I wait to make this purchase? You do not have to avoid all purchases except the absolute necessities, but it would be valuable to assess your motives and heart attitudes each time you handle money. Contentment really can be yours.

INTERACTION

On the Lighter Side

"A husband knows his wife loves him when she returns a dress he can't afford."

"There's one point at which both husband and wife are in perfect agreement—he thinks nothing is too good for her, and so does she."

"An Oklahoma woman refused to marry her boyfriend for religious reasons. He was broke, and she worshipped money."

BIBLE STUDY

MONEY

Making Sense Out of Money

Money is so much more than coins and currency. It all too often is the means by which many people rate their own personal success. And it frequently is also a source of tremendous conflict between husbands and wives.

The Bible teaches that the way people use money indicates a lot about the condition of their heart. As you complete these Bible studies, you will discover God's view of money and how it should be used. It makes sense to handle money God's way.

1. Covetousness — Hebrews 13:5

What is your conduct (or life) to be without?

What are the characteristics of a covetous person?

Describe a time in your marriage when you or your spouse exhibited covetousness.

What covetous practice most needs to be changed in your marriage?

2. Riches — 1 Timothy 6:9

What happens to those who desire to be rich?

What are some temptations generally associated with getting rich?

In your marriage, describe one temptation you have faced personally because of a desire for wealth.

How strong is your desire for riches? How strong is your mate's desire for riches?

How has the desire for riches proven to be a "snare" in your marriage?

8.6   A BIBLICAL PORTRAIT OF MARRIAGE

© 1995 by Dr. Bruce H. Wilkinson and Walk Thru the Bible Ministries, Inc. Do not reproduce.

3. Idolatry
Ephesians 5:3–5

What is a covetous man also called?

What is idolatry?

For what pleasurable activity have you had such affection that it became like an idol to you?

What has been the most devastating consequence of idolizing money in your marriage?

In your marriage, what possessions do you and your spouse need to "dethrone" from their position of prominence in your hearts?

4. Contentment
Philippians 4:11–13

When can contentment be found?

What does it mean to be content?

What three types of money decisions cause the greatest discontent and conflict between you and your spouse?

In your marriage, how have you responded when you did not have very much and were struggling to get by?

Describe a time in your marriage when God met your material needs in an extraordinary way.

5. Investments
Matthew 6:19–21

Where is treasure to be stored?

Through what types of giving can treasure be laid up in heaven?

In your marriage, what is one way you regularly invest your income in heaven?

What single change in your marriage would enable you to give more and increase your heavenly investment?

Will you resolve to learn contentment in relation to money? Will you commit yourself to increase the amount you give, share, and store up in heaven? Affirm your commitment by initialing and dating this page.

Your initials and date

DEVOTIONAL 1

The Root of the Matter

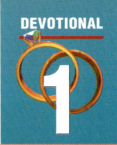

SCRIPTURE
1 Timothy 6:6–10

> For the love of money is a root of all kinds of evil, for which some have strayed from the faith in their greediness, and pierced themselves through with many sorrows.
>
> (verse 10)

"Granddad!" Dwayne called out. "I'm probably not supposed to be reading this, but it looked like kind of an old, interesting document—and I got hooked. What is it? Or, is it okay to ask?"

"Well, I'm sure it is, Dwayne. Let's see what you've got there," Bob Ethridge, Sr., said to his grandson, looking through his bifocals at the paper Dwayne handed him. "Ah, yes. This must have fallen out of that last box of files we carried upstairs. Brings back memories."

Dwayne stood silently, looking at his grandfather, then said, "If it's personal, Granddad, don't worry about it..."

"Not at all. Might be something you could think about for you and Sherry. Years ago Alice and I drew up this document, signed it, and had our pastor witness it and sign it with us. It was a way for us to make a decision about money in our marriage."

"So, what's it say, Granddad?"

"Well, it says that should the Lord ever want to use us as a channel for His resources to spread His Gospel around the world in a significant way, we're available. Alice and I agreed that if we ever unexpectedly came into a large amount of money—from whatever the source—that 75 percent of it would go immediately to the Lord's work, 20 percent to you kids' college fund, and 5 percent to cover any bills or expenses we might have at that time. Settling the 'how we'd use it' issue beforehand frees up God to decide the 'if.' It takes a lot of pressure off in the long run."

From the Word

Many years of dealing with money and knowing God had led Bob and Alice to a creative plan. When they matured to the point that "having money" was not an issue, then "using money" for godly purposes could become the goal. What they had concluded agreed with the Apostle Paul's teaching in 1 Timothy 6. Perhaps one of the most misquoted verses in Scripture, verse 10 focuses not on money but on the heart. Love, not money, is the issue. What do we love? Money is not to be an end in itself, but rather a means to an end—the end expressed in an historic catechism, "To glorify God and enjoy Him forever."

For the Heart

Do you and your spouse have a plan for your money? A thought-through and prayed-through plan can allow love for God, not lust for gain, to be reflected by your use of money.

Where does the Lord fit in your present perspective? If you haven't done so in a while, go over your finances with your spouse as if you were a stranger on the outside. Write down the three things your family "loves" most as revealed by your spending. Evaluate and discuss how you can make progress as a couple in demonstrating even more eternal values through your spending.

The root of all evil is in the heart, not the pocket or purse.

DEVOTIONAL 2

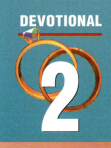

Reaping What You Sow

SCRIPTURE
2 Corinthians 9:6

But this I say: He who sows sparingly will also reap sparingly, and he who sows bountifully will also reap bountifully.

"Lillith, that's wonderful! I think that's a very mature step you've taken—and God will honor your decision." Alice was trying not to make her daughter feel self-conscious about the financial decision she had made. But inwardly, this mother was shouting *Hallelujah!*

"Tell me what led you to make your decision, dear," Alice ventured carefully.

"Well, I guess it started with a sermon Pastor Burton preached at church a few weeks ago. Maybe because I work at a bank, and the sermon had to do with money, I listened more closely. But the bottom line had to do with 'you reap what you sow.' I tend to forget that's a Bible verse instead of something by Benjamin Franklin."

"What did Pastor Burton say?" Alice was trying to act relaxed, even casual, so as not to pressure this spiritually-maturing daughter with too much, too soon.

"Well, the sermon was about when Paul was trying to get the people in a church in . . . somewhere . . . wherever . . . to send money to the church in Jerusalem. He told them that if they gave generously, they would get back generously. That caught my ROI ear—you know, Return on Investment?—and started me thinking. About money, that is."

"And . . ." Alice encouraged.

"Well, not only did I figure that giving more of what I earn to God was a good investment financially, but that maybe He would even give me more in other ways, like peace of mind."

From the Word

A paradox in God's kingdom is found in the area of finances: The blessing of receiving begins with the discipline of giving. It is indeed more blessed to give than to receive.

Drawn from the world of agriculture, where farmers reap disproportionately more than what they sow, the paradox exists for money as well. Paul explained to the Corinthian believers how God returns abundantly when we invest in the kingdom of God (see 2 Corinthians 9:6). While by the world's standard, giving away what we desire to receive sounds foolish, with God it is the standard. The motive of giving is not to get, but God does say that what we receive is tied to what we give. That is, we reap what we sow.

For the Heart

With your spouse, make a list of all the areas in which your family budget is "too little, too late"—where you could definitely use more income for legitimate necessities.

Scrutinize your list, and arrive at a dollar figure that you could, with a clear conscience, ask God to provide. Next, examine your giving. Have the pressures on your family budget kept you from giving to Him as generously as you would like? Consider increasing your giving to God as an opportunity for Him to demonstrate His faithfulness to you—and to His Word and its promises! Don't forget the paradox—give and then receive.

Giving what you can't keep to get what you can't lose is wise.

DEVOTIONAL 3

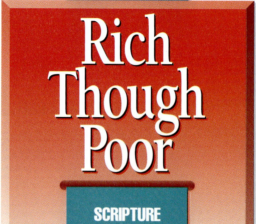

Rich Though Poor

SCRIPTURE
2 Corinthians 8:1–4

For I bear witness that according to their ability, yes, and beyond their ability, they were freely willing.

(verse 3)

"So, let me guess, hon," Bob began on their way home from church. "You're so quiet because you're planning a special Sunday lunch of liver 'n onions. Or maybe planning how you're going to rub my back for a solid hour after lunch. Or . . ."

"Wrong so far," Deb perked up. "We're having sandwiches for lunch and I wanted you to rub *my* back."

"Okay—but that's not why you're being so quiet. Something wrong?"

"Well, not really wrong. I was just amazed at Mrs. Allen in church this morning. Did you see what she did when they took the offering for the Missions Committee to help build the church in Haiti?" Deb asked.

"Hmmm. Can't say that I did. She didn't take money *out* did she?!" Bob said in mock alarm.

"No, Bob, she didn't. But she did put money *in!*" Deb exclaimed.

"Uh . . . okay, like we did, and lots of other people. I'm not following you."

"Bob," Deb turned to face him as they drove, "Mrs. Allen is an eighty-year-old widow with hardly *anything* to live on herself. She's practically destitute! In fact, when I was on the Benevolence Committee last year, we gave her money once when she had an emergency need. So when I saw her reach in her little purse and get twenty dollars out for the Mission Fund, I almost cried. I know there must be things she needs herself that she could have bought with that money. I didn't mean to look, but she was sitting right beside me."

"Twenty bucks?" Bob said. "That makes my five look a little shabby, huh?"

From the Word

Has there been a Mrs. Allen in your life? A person who contradicts all known principles of economics by living on next to nothing since most of what he or she has goes to the Lord? These people are living examples of the Macedonians, those Christians whom Paul wrote about in his second letter to the church at Corinth (8:1–4). Believers in Macedonia had begged Paul for the privilege of giving to the struggling church in Jerusalem. Though poor themselves, they gave beyond their evident ability, and substituted the riches of joy for their poverty of material wealth. They had discovered what Paul refers to as the "grace" (verse 1) of giving.

For the Heart

Everyone should experience the grace of God in giving. If, as a couple, your finances are relatively stable at the moment, you may not have the opportunity to "give out of your poverty." But perhaps you and your spouse have personal funds over which you have spending discretion that you could ask God to help you use in some unique situation.

Ask God to let you both experience, individually or as a couple, the ability to give out of your "poverty" in the next 30 days. Setting aside something you want, or even need, in order to give, is a true grace.

The hand empty from giving is never empty for very long.

DEVOTIONAL 4

Wealth and How to Get It

SCRIPTURE
Proverbs 13:11

Wealth gained by dishonesty will be diminished, but he who gathers [little by little] will increase.

"Are you kidding me? I don't believe it!" Dwayne exclaimed, sitting back in his chair to soak in the impact of what he had just seen.

He and Sherry were doing premarital counseling with the associate pastor at Sherry's church where they would soon be married.

Rick Edison, the associate pastor, had just shown them a graph on the power of compounding interest on money over time. He was trying to illustrate for them the Biblical principle of saving "little by little" as an act of responsible stewardship for married couples.

"Wow! You mean we could save that small amount each year for less than ten years and end up with nearly a million bucks when we retire? You sure that's right, Rick?" Dwayne asked.

Laughing, Rick assured them it was right, explaining why compound interest is called the "Eighth Wonder of the World."

"The big question is not whether it works, but whether you will allow it to work for *you*," Rick continued. "Look at it this way. When you two marry and set up a budget, it will reflect three decisions if it is Biblical. Number one, you'll take the Lord's portion right off the top every month. Second, you'll pay your taxes, though that's normally handled by your employer unless you're self-employed. But thirdly—and this is the hard one—you need to take a percentage right off the top every month to save for the future—you know, like retirement, emergencies, or whatever comes up."

From the Word

For most Christians, the first half of Proverbs 13:11 is not a big problem. That is, most people don't acquire wealth dishonestly. The larger problem is that most people never acquire any wealth at all! And by "wealth" we are not talking about millions of dollars. Rather, wealth in a Biblical sense is simply that reserve that is stored away, "little by little." It is prudent and wise to accumulate wealth on a regular basis to prepare for unexpected emergencies and to supplement income in the latter years of life. Acquiring wealth through saving is not hoarding, it is not greed, and it is not with the intent of growing rich. It is the steady exercise of self-discipline for the meeting of future needs.

For the Heart

Do you and your spouse save on a regular basis? If you are like most couples, you may not be saving enough, as much as you should, or any at all.

Take stock of your current saving strategy. Have you grown dependent on credit cards to meet emergency financial needs? Perhaps you need to open a savings account, and have the monthly amount drafted from your checking account as a way to begin. Starting by saving something each month will encourage you to continue as your savings grow.

Little-by-little will eventually become a-lot-by-a-lot more!

DEVOTIONAL

5

From Surprise to Sorrow

SCRIPTURE
Proverbs 10:22

The blessing of the Lord makes one rich, and He adds no sorrow with it.

"Bob!" Deb shrieked. "Come here!" Expecting the worst, Bob dropped his Saturday lunch sandwich in the middle of his plate, pushed back from the table and bounded for the foyer where Deb had the mail.

"What is it, Deb?" he gasped, rounding the corner.

"I'll tell you what it is! It's seven hundred, forty-five dollars, and thirty-six cents! THAT'S what it is! Can you believe it? Thank you, Lord!"

"Let me see that, Deb," Bob said with heightened interest. He began to read the letter that accompanied the check, discovering it was from the mortgage company through which they had recently refinanced their house.

"Oh, I get it," he said exhaling. "It's a refund from our escrow account on the house. It says that after we refinanced, they discovered an error in the loan papers and they're refunding an excess in the account. Not bad. Not bad at all . . ." Bob said vacantly as he began to walk back toward the kitchen.

"Bob! Wait! Where are you going with that check?!" Deb asked aggressively. Her tone surprised Bob.

"Well, I guess I wasn't going anywhere—except to finish my sandwich. What's the problem?"

"Uh, well, I mean, what are you—I mean WE—going to do with the money? We really need to replace that thread-bare sofa in the living room with a sleeper sofa—and pillows and drapes."

"Deb, be serious. You and I both need new tires on our cars, and mine needs a major tune-up. This check will just about cover it."

From the Word

Oops! Sounds like Saturday was a better day *before* the mail arrived! At least Bob and Deb weren't on the verge of an argument.

Here's a good test to apply to money in marriage: Is money a source of blessing or a source of tension? In other words, are we better off with it or without it, spiritually and relationally speaking? Scripture is clear that it is the Lord who generously blesses His children with riches—whether the amounts are large or small. But Scripture is also clear that if money creates division or sorrow, then a power other than God's is at work—the power of greed. Don't let monetary surprises produce marital sorrows!

For the Heart

Stop and think: When was the last time a sum of money was the source of conflict in your marriage?

Try to make a list of the times and reasons money has been problematic in your marriage, and see how many were because of violations of other Scriptural principles. For example, did the wife not follow the husband's leadership? Was the husband uncommunicative? Perhaps greedy? Try to identify the root causes of financial conflict and purpose to submit to God's principles. And then *enjoy* God's financial blessing to the fullest!

When riches produce strife, they are no longer riches at all.

SESSION 9

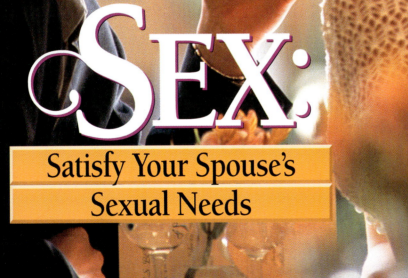

SEX:
Satisfy Your Spouse's Sexual Needs

Sex within its intended domain of marriage is a special gift from God. But even within marriage sex can fail to satisfy if it has lost its passion, its affection, and its pleasure. Restore all three in *your* marriage. ■

CLASS NOTES

SEX:
Satisfy Your Spouse's Sexual Needs

INTRODUCTION

_____
_____
_____
_____

What are some key Scriptures that present God's view of sex in marriage?

_____ _____

_____ _____

How does 1 Corinthians 7:2–5 instruct husbands and wives about satisfying one's spouse sexually?

1. Sexual needs are to be met _____ your marriage.

2. God commands you to _____ your spouse's sexual needs.

3. Fulfill your spouse's sexual needs _____ and _____.

_____
_____

9.2 A BIBLICAL PORTRAIT OF MARRIAGE

© 1995 by Dr. Bruce H. Wilkinson and Walk Thru the Bible Ministries, Inc. Do not reproduce.

4. God delegates _____ over your body to your _____.

   Your body is for your spouse's _____.

5. Abstaining from sex is permissible only if _____ spouses _____.

6. _____ sexual relations with your spouse after the agreed time apart.

7. God warns of _____ sexual temptation if sex is _____.

What should a person do to "possess his own vessel in sanctification and honor" (1 Thessalonians 4:3–8)?

1. _____ have sex _____ of marriage.
2. _____ _____ from yielding to immoral temptation.
3. Learn how to _____ your own sex drive.
4. Tell your _____ how your sexual drives can be _____.

CONCLUSION

_____

_____

EVALUATION

Sex: Satisfy Your Spouse's Sexual Needs

Are you experiencing a gratifying and fulfilling sexual relationship with your spouse? Just a reminder: Score this evaluation according to what is generally true at this time in your marriage.

God made men and women very different. And how you and your spouse view sex in your marriage may be very different as well. Purpose to openly and respectfully discuss how you might better satisfy your spouse's sexual needs.

Couples, how satisfying is sex in your marriage?
Total your score below.

		False		Sometimes				True
A	Both of us are committed to meeting each other's sexual needs.	1	2	3	4	5	6	7
B	Our enjoyment before, during, and after sex is enhanced by the tenderness and affection we express to each other.	1	2	3	4	5	6	7
C	Sex is pleasurable and satisfying for both of us.	1	2	3	4	5	6	7
D	We discuss and agree upon any temporary abstinence from sex.	1	2	3	4	5	6	7
E	We do not give or withhold sex as a means of retaliation, manipulation, or control.	1	2	3	4	5	6	7
F	Both of us have learned how to manage our own sex drives and express those drives appropriately within our marriage.	1	2	3	4	5	6	7
G	We do not yield to immorality or any expression of our sexuality outside of marriage.	1	2	3	4	5	6	7
H	We feel comfortable talking with each other about our sexual relationship.	1	2	3	4	5	6	7

Column Subtotals:

The Couple's "Sex" Score
- **48–56 G** = Great sex!
- **38–47 PG** = Pretty Good sex!
- **28–37 PG-13** = Potentially Good sex.
- **18–27 R** = Recommend more sex.
- **8–17 X** = Extra effort suggested.

GRAND TOTAL:

INTERACTION

1 How is sex generally portrayed through the media today? How does the media usually present sex within marriage?

2 How are the human body and sex within marriage depicted in the Scriptures? How does the Bible speak of sex outside of marriage?

3 How was the subject of sex dealt with in your family? Complete the following statement: "Growing up, I felt sex was..."

4 Why is it often so difficult to discuss sex with the person you love the most?

5 What would a person have to know about his or her spouse in order to most effectively communicate love through sex?

On the Lighter Side

"What makes a great lover? A great lover is someone who can satisfy one woman over a lifetime ... and who can be satisfied by one woman all his life long. A great lover is not someone who goes from woman to woman to woman. Any dog can do that."
—An American film actor

"A wife is not a guitar; you can't play on her and then hang her on the wall."
—Russian proverb

PROJECT: SATISFY YOUR SPOUSE SEXUALLY

Approach this project with gentleness, humility, and sincerity. Each of you should **rate** your sexual satisfaction on a scale from 1 to 10 (1 = Unsatisfied and 10 = Very Satisfied). **Discuss** your ratings as well as some of the following: what you most enjoy about sex with your spouse, what makes you uncomfortable, how much tender affection and conversation you prefer, how often you need sex, at what times you most need to engage in sex, what attitudes expressed during the day by your spouse make it difficult to enjoy sex, and what nonverbal sexual clues you and your spouse communicate to each other. **Tell** your spouse what he or she could do to make sex more enjoyable for you.

BIBLE STUDY

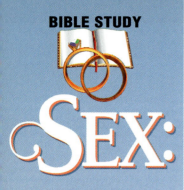

SEX:

For Your Enjoyment

Sex was God's idea. And among other things, He intended it for pleasure. While man has often corrupted God's design, God's pure and joyful intent still remains.

Scripture provides numerous illustrations and exhortations regarding the proper and improper ways to express one's sexuality. The focus of these studies will be the positive expression of one's sex drive within marriage.

These questions are based on clear Biblical teaching, but they are rather direct. Since this course workbook is not like a lockable diary, you might want to be discreet in what you write down (or perhaps write your answers on a separate sheet of paper).

1 Sex is Good — Hebrews 13:4

How is sex in marriage described in this verse?

Why do many people view sex as shameful or dirty?

What practices within marriage might indicate that you or your spouse see sex as something disgraceful?

How do you view sex personally?

2 Sexual Affection — 1 Corinthians 7:2–3

How are husbands and wives to respond to one another sexually?

What does the word "affection" imply?

What do you most appreciate about how your spouse renders sexual affection to you?

What do you wish your spouse would do differently so that sex would be more enjoyable for you?

What could you do to make sex more meaningful for your spouse?

3. Avoid Excuses
1 Corinthians 7:4–5

Who holds the rights to your body according to this passage?

What are some of the most common excuses given for not wanting to have sex?

What excuse does your spouse give that frustrates you the most?

What alibi have you used that you know disappointed—and maybe even angered—your spouse?

In what types of situations in your marriage would it be appropriate for you to surrender your right to have sex?

4. Sexual Purity
1 Thessalonians 4:4

What instruction is given in verse 4 about how to "possess" your own body?

How can a person keep his or her body and heart pure?

List three characteristics of your own sex drive and sexual needs.

What is the most important strategy you could implement to be sensitive to your own sex drive?

5. Pleasure in Sex
Proverbs 5:18–19

What should be true of a married couple's sexual relationship?

Why should such joy and pleasure only be possible within marriage?

How could you convey to your mate today your commitment to discover and continue experiencing great pleasure in sex?

Will you submit your body to your spouse for his or her pleasure? Will you commit yourself to satisfying your mate's sexual needs? Signify your commitment by initialing and dating this page.

Your initials and date

Sex: Satisfy Your Spouse's Sexual Needs

DEVOTIONAL

The Bible Says We Have To?

**SCRIPTURE
1 Corinthians 7:2–5**

Do not deprive one another except with consent for a time, that you may give yourselves to fasting and prayer; and come together again so that Satan does not tempt you because of your lack of self-control.

(verse 5)

At 2:00 A.M., Bob was sure that his tiptoes were echoing through the house like a bass drum. And then he saw what he dreaded most: a crack of light under the bedroom door. *Oh man,* he thought. *Deb's still up.*

Quietly turning the doorknob, Bob peeked in. Sure enough, Deb was sitting up in bed, watching an old movie on T.V. Her lack of greeting was his first clue that her mind was on more than the movie.

"Hi, hon," he managed meekly. (No response.)

"What'cha watchin'?" came the second attempt. (Still no response.)

While brushing his teeth, Bob heard the T.V. go off. *Okay, Bob. Be patient. Let her talk,* Bob began mentally coaching himself.

"I can't take much more of this overtime, Bob," Deb began, still staring straight ahead. "This has been going on for two weeks now. You haven't been home before midnight once. I don't think I have a husband anymore—not to mention the kids having a father."

"I know, Deb. I think we're at the end of the tunnel. The new machines are installed, and we're just trying to get the bugs out. I've about had it myself. But I think maybe one or two more late nights should wrap it up."

A tear escaped Deb's eye. "If I wanted to sleep by myself, Bob, I would have stayed single. I have needs that can only be met in this bed, by you—which means you have to be here! But if you're not here, those needs don't get met. And I'm tired of feeling guilty about wanting what I believe is normal. Can you understand that?"

From the Word

Bob would understand Deb more clearly if he had read Paul's admonitions in 1 Corinthians 7:2–5. But given his schedule, not only had he been missing regular times of intimacy with Deb, he probably hadn't been reading his Bible very much either!

Paul clearly says that the meeting of our spouse's sexual needs are a top priority in marriage. We know this because of his warning that Satan stands ready to tempt those who are not being satisfied sexually by their spouse. Temptations to immorality or carnality are all possible dangers couples face. In verse 3, Paul has instructions for Bob: Do not deprive one another sexually.

For the Heart

The goal in this week's devotions is for you and your spouse to affirm your commitments to satisfying one another sexually.

Because the rewards are great in this area of marriage, so are the risks. Different preferences, personality factors, parental influences—even a lack of time to relax—all work against a couple's "sexual satisfaction score."

But you can change all that—this week! Whether you have been married two weeks or twenty years, stop and pray that your heart would be open to meeting your spouse's needs sexually—and vice versa!

How to keep temptation from your marriage: Have sex regularly!

DEVOTIONAL 2

Two Sides to Every Coin

SCRIPTURE
Malachi 2:15a

But did He not make them one . . . ? And why one? He seeks godly offspring.

"So, what are your thoughts on sex?" Pastor Rick Edison suddenly asked with a big grin on his face.

"We're for it!" Dwayne shot back without batting an eye.

"Dwayne!" Sherry exclaimed, her red face revealing an embarrassment at her fiancé's answer.

The associate pastor of Sherry's church had started off this session of the young couple's premarital counseling with a bang. And got what he was looking for—a spontaneous measure of their comfort level with the subject.

"Okay, Casanova," Rick continued, "while Sherry loses some of the color in her cheeks, tell me what you think the purpose of sex in marriage is. That is, why are you so enthusiastically 'for it'?"

"Uh, well, you know, it's supposed to be for husbands and wives, right?, to express their love for one another, and uh, to enjoy themselves, you know, to have a good time, legal-like, in God's sight? Am I right?" Dwayne hoped so.

"We'll see . . . How about you, Sherry? What do you think sex is for?" Pastor Edison said, turning to Sherry.

"Well, I guess I agree with what Dwayne said, but I thought it's mostly for having children. I mean, in the Garden of Eden there were no birth control methods, were there? So sex is mainly for 'being fruitful and multiplying,' it seems to me."

"Good answers," Pastor Edison said. "You're both describing separate sides of the same coin. But I want to find out if you can understand and agree with each other's perspective."

From the Word
There are many couples who do not enter marriage with the same views on the purpose of sex—or on many other aspects of sexuality in marriage. And until those different views are surfaced, discussed, and hopefully blended or reconciled, potential is high for hurt and disappointment.

Malachi 2:15a is at least one verse which seems to address both Dwayne's and Sherry's thoughts. God has made couples "one," and it is true that the "physical" aspects of sexuality are very pleasurable indeed. And yet Malachi also says that God desired a godly offspring. He wanted the pleasure of sex to encourage married couples to have sex often—to populate the earth. So both views, in Malachi's view, are correct!

For the Heart
In your marriage, how would each of you have answered Pastor Edison's question? There is a good way to find out!

You and your spouse should jot down the three best reasons you can each think of for cultivating and practicing sex within marriage. Then rank them (1 = top reason, 3 = last). But don't let your spouse see your answer!

Then swap lists, and see how close you were to each other. The point is not to agree exactly, but to talk, and learn together, to strengthen the sexual side of your marriage.

Being fruitful and multiplying is a genuine pleasure.

DEVOTIONAL 3

Better After Fifty

SCRIPTURE
Song of Solomon 7:10–13

Let us get up early to the vineyards; let us see if the vine has budded, whether the grape blossoms are open, and the pomegranates are in bloom. There I will give you my love.

(verse 12)

It was the perfect conclusion to a perfect anniversary for Bob and Alice. A romantic restaurant overlooking a lake near town had put them in a reminiscing mood. Alice wondered out loud what kind of sexual standards Dwayne and Sherry had been able to maintain for themselves during their engagement.

"Granted," Bob reflected, "we remained pure before marriage. But I bet the kind of lovemaking you and I did once we were married was every bit as 'with it' as young marrieds today, don't you think?"

Alice looked down at her plate modestly, caught off guard by Bob's remark. But she recovered quickly: "I think we could probably show the young folks a thing or two still. IN FACT, Bob, that reminds me..." Alice said a bit dreamily.

"Of what?" Bob asked, puzzled—but a bit energized by Alice's tone.

"Well, in my devotions this week, my Bible reading schedule took me to the Song of Solomon. And there's a passage in chapter seven—I just read it today—about the bride and her husband going to the vineyards, where she says to him, 'I will give you my love.' Now who do I know that has a large vineyard in their backyard, totally concealed with vines and leaves this time of year, that would be absolutely private on this dark night? Hmmm?"

"Why, Alice! I guess that would be me. I mean, it would be *us!* Yes, we *do* have a vineyard, don't we? Ah, why exactly did you ask, young lady?"

"Well, the night's still young, and I think we are too, . . . aren't we?"

From the Word

From the early church to the modern church, not a few Christians have blushed at the plain language of the Song of Solomon. Yes, it is mature language; but yes, love is a mature subject. Problems come when allegedly mature couples don't talk maturely about sex—like the Song of Solomon does. Chapter 7, verse 12, contains one of many forthright statements of the desire and the delight of married love. Marital sex is pictured in this book of the Bible as a celebration of godly pleasures. It compares sex and love in marriage to all of the delightful pleasures in God's creation. Satisfied will be the couple who sings this Song together.

For the Heart

Plan a time with your spouse to read the Song of Solomon together. Will it sound unusual? Most likely, because most people don't talk in poetic verse form. Will it be uncomfortable? Possibly, because most couples are not used to expressing their love verbally for one another. But therein lies the benefit. Reading the Song of Solomon together will perhaps loosen, or at least pinpoint, some inhibitions which have set in over time in your marriage.

And when you are through reading, look around for a vineyard!

They say sex is even better after fifty. Or was it sixty? Or seventy?

DEVOTIONAL 4

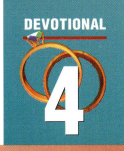

Just Say No. Then Flee!

SCRIPTURE
1 Corinthians 6:12–19

Flee sexual immorality. Every sin that a man does is outside the body, but he who commits sexual immorality sins against his own body.
(verse 18)

When Pastor Burton answered his phone, he was surprised to hear Larry greet him. And even more surprised at his request—though it was one he was glad to address.

"Thanks for taking my call, Pastor," Larry began. "I know this is going to sound a bit weird, but I need some help in a couple of ways."

"Whatever I can do, Larry, I will. I'm delighted you called," Dan Burton offered. "What's up?"

"Well, I've got a problem at work. There's a single girl who works in my department who has become overly friendly toward me ever since Lillith and I divorced. In fact, that's putting it mildly. She's made it pretty clear to me, verbally and otherwise, that she's available for—well, whatever. There was a time in my life that I would have loved this kind of 'problem,' but I really am trying to do things differently now."

"I see," Dan replied. "What's your response been? And how can I help?"

"So far, I've resisted her. She's very attractive, but I doubt if she's a Christian. I'm just not interested in a relationship right now," Larry said.

"I understand. I think you're wise on that count. But let me get down to the bottom line: Are you asking for help in resisting the temptation to become physically involved with this woman? Is that what you're asking?"

"Yeah—I guess so. I mean, I know it would be wrong in God's sight, and I want to do what's right. But man, it's tempting. Do you know what I mean? I guess I just need somebody to get in my face and yell 'NO WAY' real loud."

From the Word

Larry came to the right place as long as Pastor Burton turned to 1 Corinthians 6:18. The Apostle Paul makes no compromises about a Christian's responsibility in times of inappropriate sexual temptation: FLEE! And fast! One wonders if Paul had the example of Joseph in mind from the Old Testament (see Genesis 39). If you recall the story, Joseph literally fled from the place of sexual temptation in which he found himself. And a wise decision it was. Regardless of gender or marital status, the Bible is perfectly clear that the Christian's duty is to flee sexual immorality—energetically, purposefully, and decisively. It is not always easy or convenient—but it is always required.

For the Heart

The problem with sexual temptation—mental *or* physical—is how subtly it can appear. It can happen in your neighborhood, at church, in the workplace—wherever! The best defense? Accountability and communication—like Larry initiated as a single man with his pastor.

Have you and your spouse discussed this issue together? It requires transparency and humility—how will you respond if your spouse admits to being sexually tempted by another? Have a careful, graceful, and gentle conversation about this topic—with your pastor, if needed.

A temptation admitted is a temptation partially conquered.

DEVOTIONAL 5

Put Sleepin' In on Your To-Do List

SCRIPTURE
Proverbs 5:15–23

Drink water from your own cistern, and running water from your own well. (verse 15)

"Sarah, you look like a kitten that just finished a *big* bowl of milk," Betty teased her best friend Sarah. "Come on in. Have you had lunch yet?"

These two women met at least weekly to stay in touch, and this Saturday it was lunch at Betty's. Since college, theirs had been a no-secrets kind of relationship.

"So, you didn't answer my question. Why the look of contentment? Or am I overstating the situation?" Betty asked genuinely.

"Not really. Maybe understating if you want to know the truth. I know it's noon, but I just got up a while ago. Jack and I stayed in bed the whole morning since both kids spent the night with friends. To be honest, I'm drained—but a good kind of drained, if you get my drift. And you haven't missed my drift often in the last fifteen years, have you?" Sarah giggled.

"No, I haven't, especially today. And it sounds wonderful!" Betty said with a hint of envy. "I'm glad you had such a fun time together."

Their mutual, momentary silence set the stage for a serious next word.

"Betty, how do you handle not having any physical intimacy? I mean, Will died years ago—that's a long time to sleep alone every night. Do you mind me asking?" Sarah inquired.

"Of course not," Betty opened up. "It's not easy sometimes. I live in the memory of how much Will cherished our physical intimacy. It was so special. I guess I'm still not to the point where I ever want to experience that with anyone but him. Does that make sense?"

From the Word

Perhaps living in the past is not always a healthy thing, but one can understand Betty's sentiment. To be totally cherished and honored in the sexual realm is a unique experience in our world of devolving standards and one-night stands. And, it is thoroughly Biblical. In Proverbs 5:15–23, a father gives his son advice about avoiding sexual immorality. The defensive strategy is to be aware of the adulteress and her deceitful schemes. The offensive strategy is to rejoice in and cherish the wife of one's youth. The wife is compared to a cistern of water—a valuable, highly protected, and life-giving resource. In other words, a prized possession.

For the Heart

How cherished and prized is the sexual intimacy that you share with your spouse? When a windfall of free time appears, is it ever spent in a lovingly relaxed time of intimacy instead of tackling the "to-do" list of household chores?

"Cherishing" does not happen naturally. In fact, given the natural course of events, all things will become "less cherished" over time unless extra effort is exerted.

Consider surprising your spouse soon with a special time of intimacy together. After all, you know the chores will still be there tomorrow.

Some Saturday morning "chores" are more enjoyable than others!

SESSION **10**

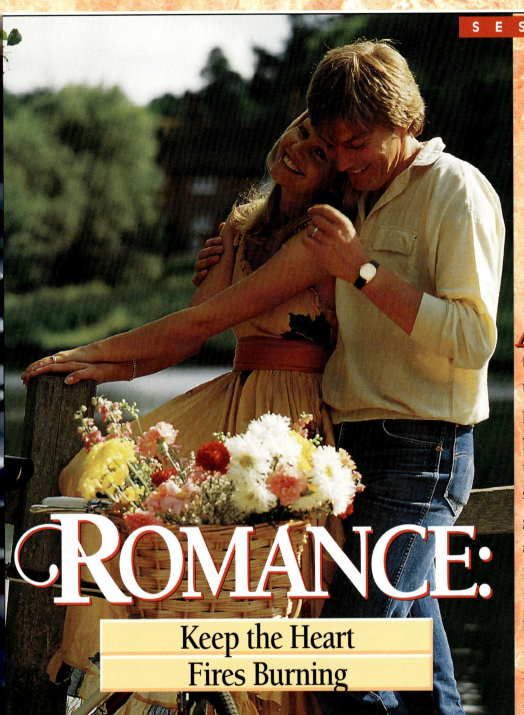

ROMANCE:

Keep the Heart Fires Burning

All too often, romance begins to vanish in the post-wedding years. It is not usually lost suddenly, but gradually fades away over time. Learn to keep the heart fires burning as you make the latter years even more romantic than the first! ■

ROMANCE:
Keep the Heart Fires Burning

INTRODUCTION

_____
_____
_____
_____
_____

What are the most common lies people believe about romance?

1. I _____ _____ of love.

2. I married the _____ person.

3. I've tried and tried. I _____ _____.

4. I'm too _____ and _____.

5. Everyone knows, romance always _____.

6. My spouse can't love me the way I _____ to be loved.

7. It's just _____ _____ to be.

_____
_____
_____

For what reasons might a couple experience the loss of romantic love?

1. Refusal to _____ your spouse (Ephesians 4:32).

2. Refusal to _____ the spouse God _____ you to be.

What universal principles express the truth about romance?

1. _____ your marriage (Genesis 2:24).

2. Assume your _____ (Genesis 2:18; Ephesians 5:23).

3. Fulfill your _____ (Colossians 3:18–19).

4. _____ sexual affection (1 Corinthians 7:2–5).

5. Become incredibly _____ (1 Peter 3:3–4, 7).

6. Love in _____ _____.

7. _____ and do the first _____ (Revelation 2:4–5).

CONCLUSION

_____

_____

_____

EVALUATION

Romance: Keep the Heart Fires Burning

Husbands and wives may have very diverse perspectives on what is considered romantic. But true romance, while it includes things you do, grows out of right heart attitudes.

Take this evaluation to see if romance is alive and well in your marriage.

Evaluate the ongoing expression of romantic love in your marriage. Total your score below.

		False			Sometimes			True
A	We are still very much in love and the expression of romantic love is strong in our marriage.	1	2	3	4	5	6	7
B	We have both learned how to express romantic love in ways that are particularly meaningful to each other.	1	2	3	4	5	6	7
C	Neither of us has closed parts of our heart from our spouse through unforgiveness or bitterness.	1	2	3	4	5	6	7
D	With God's help we are committed to being the kind of spouses God has commanded us to be.	1	2	3	4	5	6	7
E	The husband's heart is drawn to the wife through her gentle and quiet spirit.	1	2	3	4	5	6	7
F	The wife is romantically attracted to the husband because of the way he honors and cares for her.	1	2	3	4	5	6	7
G	We enjoy a wonderful friendship. We truly enjoy being together and doing things together.	1	2	3	4	5	6	7
H	We experience true spiritual oneness in our marriage because we both know Christ as Savior.	1	2	3	4	5	6	7

Column Subtotals:

The Couple's "Romance" Score
- **48–56** Dinner cruise on the Seine, *ma chérie*.
- **38–47** Picnic by the lake.
- **28–37** Frozen TV dinners with candles.
- **18–27** Potluck dinner with the in-laws.
- **8–17** Coupon night at Dave's Chili Beanery.

GRAND TOTAL:

1 How does modern-day society portray femininity and masculinity? How do these portrayals differ from Scripture's perspective?

2 What kinds of things does the typical wife think are romantic? What is considered romantic by most husbands?

3 How could romance be defined? What makes it different from love?

4 What are the most common hindrances to sustaining romantic love in marriage?

5 As you have observed couples who are still romantically in love, how would you describe them? How do they act around each other?

PROJECT: LEARN TO BE ROMANTIC AGAIN

Rekindling romance in your marriage is based on forgiveness and an obedience to God's instruction. But it is also re-learned through practice. Choose one or both of the following options. **Option #1: Start dating again.** What do you enjoy doing together? Picnics or the symphony or boating or biking or tennis or _____ (fill in the blank). **Option #2: Say "I love you" creatively.** How did you do this before you were married? Notes or cards or phone calls or flowers or _____ (fill in the blank). Re-introduce romance to your relationship and don't allow "real life" to interrupt romance again.

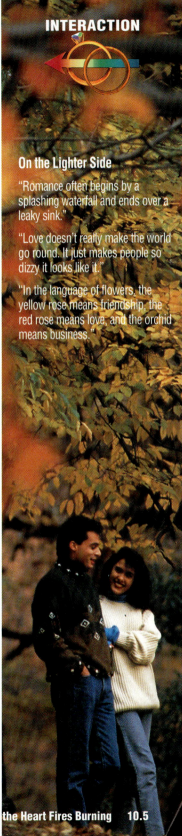

INTERACTION

On the Lighter Side

"Romance often begins by a splashing waterfall and ends over a leaky sink."

"Love doesn't really make the world go round. It just makes people so dizzy it looks like it."

"In the language of flowers, the yellow rose means friendship, the red rose means love, and the orchid means business."

BIBLE STUDY

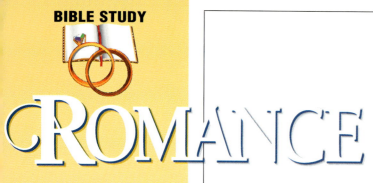

ROMANCE

Where Did All the Romance Go?

Who can forget the feelings associated with first being in love? The pleasure of seeing that special someone? The delight in just being together? The happiness found in hearing the words, "I love you"?

That kind of romance can be yours again as you seek to live in your marriage according to God's principles. In these studies, discover how God's truth can impact you personally.

1 Love's Depth
Song of Solomon 8:6–7

What word pictures are used to describe the lasting nature of romantic love?

How does a man or woman respond to this kind of declaration of love?

How does your spouse let you know that he or she has a deep romantic love for you?

How could you stir the flames of romantic love in your marriage?

2 A Woman's Beauty
1 Peter 3:3–4

On what type of beauty is the woman to focus her efforts?

What is a gentle and quiet spirit?

In your marriage, what percentage of time does the wife spend on outward beauty? What kind of effort does she expend on the cultivation of inner beauty?

How does the wife visibly demonstrate inner beauty?

In what one way would the husband most value the wife exhibiting gentleness and meekness?

3. A Man's Respect
1 Peter 3:7

How is the husband to relate to his wife according to this verse?

Why should the husband give honor to his wife?

What hinders some men from being gracious and respectful to their wives?

In your marriage, how does the husband treat the wife with courtesy and consideration?

In what one way would the wife most appreciate the husband's respect and understanding?

4. Loss of Love
Revelation 2:4

What did God have against the Ephesian church?

What are two or three common evidences that a couple has "left their first love"?

In your marriage, how have you been tempted to forsake your commitment to love your spouse?

How have you and your spouse worked at maintaining depth in your love relationship?

What needs to change in your life for you to see a revival of an affectionate, romantic love for your spouse?

5. Love's Memory
Revelation 2:5

What does Jesus instruct the Ephesians to do in this verse?

As you reflect and remember the early days in your courtship, what first attracted you to your spouse?

What are three happy memories from the days when you and your spouse first fell in love?

What would you most like your spouse to do with or for you that he or she did when your romance began?

Will you faithfully endeavor to be the spouse God intends you to be so that you can experience true romance in your marriage? Demonstrate your heartfelt commitment to romantically love your spouse by initialing and dating this page.

Your initials and date

DEVOTIONAL 1

A Card-Carrying Romantic

SCRIPTURE
Isaiah 5:1–2

My Well-beloved has a vineyard on a very fruitful hill. He dug it up and cleared out its stones, and planted it with the choicest vine. He built a tower in its midst, and also made a winepress in it.

(verses 1b–2a)

"Hey, hey, Bob! What's this? You going in the greeting card business or what?" Bob, Jr.'s, friend at work, Jim, had wandered into his office at lunch. "Let's see what we have here," Jim continued, looking through the stack of cards on Bob's desk. "We got some 'thank you's' and some 'miss you's' and some 'I love you's.' This is real sweet, Bob. You going to bake some brownies to go with these?"

"No, but I'm betting that Deb will keep my lunch full of brownies after getting a couple of these cards. You had any fresh brownies in *your* lunch lately, Jimbo?" Bob was taking back the offensive.

"All these cards are for Deb? You in some kind of trouble?" Jim said seriously, pulling up a chair.

"No trouble. That's the whole point. These keep me out of trouble," Bob said, looking at Jim's blank stare. "You're not getting it, are you?"

"Not yet, but I'm hooked. Go on."

"Look, Jim. I learned a long time ago that a steady stream of small, romantic gestures—you know, like surprises—goes a long way in my marriage. Deb likes cards, so I send her cards. Every four or five months I hit the card shop and stock up on a dozen or so different cards. I keep some stamps in my drawer here, and send a card out to Deb every now and then. She loves it. The cards sort of add a little unexpected romance to her day! Maybe you ought to try it with Barb."

"You kidding? You want her to have a heart attack right beside the mailbox?"

From the Word

Think it's safe to assume old Jimbo hasn't had any brownies in his lunch lately?

If he were wise, he would take Bob's advice. Bob is following a pattern that was established by God—a pattern of nurturing a relationship. On the human side, we would call it "keeping romance alive." The Prophet Isaiah describes how God cultivated, over time, His relationship with the nation of Israel. Picturing Israel as a vineyard, Isaiah says that God removed the stones, turned the ground, planted a choice vine, and erected a tower for protection and a winepress for production. In other words, God nurtured Israel the way a vinedresser does a vineyard.

For the Heart

If you or your spouse were grapevines, how productive would you be based on the amount of romantic nurturing that goes on in your marriage? Would you be robust, juicy grapes, full of romantic life, or dried and shriveled raisins?

It is natural in marriages for the romance factor to diminish over time. It must be nurtured to remain high. The normal demands on both spouses' limited resources often leave little left for romance.

Nurture the romance in your marriage in a small way this week. But please—no heart attacks!

The wine of love flows sweet where roots of romance run deep.

DEVOTIONAL 2

Don't Fall for a Counterfeit

SCRIPTURE: Proverbs 7:16–18

I have spread my bed with tapestry, colored coverings of Egyptian linen. I have perfumed my bed with myrrh, aloes, and cinnamon. Come, let us take our fill of love until morning; let us delight ourselves with love.

I want to talk about something this week that might sound boring—you probably think you know all about it. But actually, it's so important and profound, it might save your marriage from destruction someday. You interested?"

Pastor Rick Edison was baiting Dwayne and Sherry to get them interested in the premarital topic he had for them that day.

"Sure," Dwayne said. "We're here to learn, Rick. What's the topic?"

"The topic is . . . Romance!" Rick announced with fanfare.

"Romance?" Dwayne said, winking at Sherry. "You're right, Rick—we've got that one covered. I mean, do Sherry and I look like we're *not* in love?"

Rick looked serious as he answered, "No, just the opposite. So do most couples who have sat where you're sitting right now. But they don't always stay that way. What I want you to see is that the number one danger for couples after being married a few years is the loss of romance in their relationship. They let the very thing that helped draw them to each other fade over time. There is an excitement, an electricity, in new relationships that can be dangerous. That romantic energy can pull married people away from their spouses to someone new if they don't keep the romance factor high in their own marriage."

Rick continued, "What is it that draws a husband to a prostitute? Or a wife to another man? It's usually some cheap and temporarily exciting counterfeit of a good thing: Romance!"

From the Word

Counterfeit romance is pictured in Proverbs 7:16–18, where a harlot lures a foolish young man off the street into her home. Should we be surprised? She has used every romantic advantage to capture his heart: a beautifully decorated bedroom, a perfumed bed, a promise of pleasure, enticing speech, and flattering lips. It is no sin for a husband or wife to be attracted to romantic gestures—as long as they are initiated by his or her spouse. But romance, like many of God's good and perfect gifts, can be used for good or evil. Husbands and wives should work hard to make their own romantic gestures so pleasing and attractive to each other that neither ever gives a counterfeit a second look.

For the Heart

You and your spouse can easily assess your potential to be attracted to another person. Discuss areas of your marriage such as efforts to maintain physical attractiveness, personal habits, romantic efforts previously undertaken but no longer practiced, frequency of "exciting" or "passionate" events in your intimate life, how often you enjoy "fun" outings together.

If you find many of these areas have fallen significantly below previous levels in your marriage, you should be on your guard. Put romance back—to guard your hearts!

Romance: One of God's tools for keeping hearts and bodies home!

DEVOTIONAL 3

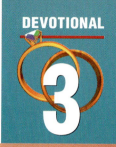

How Do I Like Thee?

SCRIPTURE
Song of Solomon 5:16b

This is my beloved, and this is my friend, O daughters of Jerusalem!

"Men, I want to suggest to you that there is a question your wives want to ask you which most of you have never even thought of." Bob, Jr., and thirty other men from the church were listening to a speaker at the annual men's retreat. He had just grabbed their attention—big time!

"In spite of the fact that you don't know the question," the speaker continued, "you are giving your wife the answer every day in numerous ways. I guarantee that your wife is processing your answers daily, even though she herself may not know how to verbalize the question mentally. But emotionally, she knows the question, and in her soul, she knows whether the answers you are giving are the answers she's looking for."

Wow, Bob thought, *what's he talking about? I'm giving Deb answers to a question that I don't know, and she might not know, even though she knows whether the answer is the right one or not? I paid fifty bucks to travel to the mountains and be confused?*

Bob began mentally drifting toward a meeting he had planned for Monday morning at the plant, outlining the agenda, when the speaker suddenly set the hook and began reeling him in.

"And the reason this question is so important for you to understand is that it sets the stage for her ability to respond romantically—that's 'sexually,' to you. Now that I've got your attention, here's the question your wife wants a positive answer to: 'Honey, I know you love me, but do you *like* me, too?'"

From the Word

Is that a Biblical question to ask? And is there a required Biblical answer? Do you have to "like" your spouse as well as love him or her?

A good place to begin would be in Song of Solomon 5:16b, where the Shulamite bride says of her husband, "This is my beloved [the one who loves me], and this is my friend [the one who likes me as well]." While love is definitely the critical issue in marriage, the question of "liking" one's spouse—cultivating a genuine friendship within marriage—probably has more to do with romance than anything else. Can you be romantic around someone who says, "I don't really like you very much"? Not very easily.

For the Heart

The mandate from God for spouses to love one another unconditionally includes being romantic—by faith, if necessary. But why make it difficult? Expressions of friendship in marriage go a long way toward "voluntary" romance in marriage.

How would your mate answer the question, "Does your spouse like you—really like to be with you as a friend as well as a marriage partner?" If you're not sure, start communicating today to your spouse, by faith, if necessary, that you like—and love—him or her as a person!

Jesus said, "I no longer call you disciples, but my friends."

DEVOTIONAL 4

You Are Hereby Invited

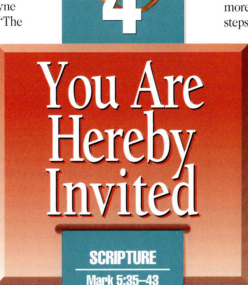

SCRIPTURE
Mark 5:35–43

And He permitted no one to follow Him except Peter, James, and John. . . . But when He had put [the crowd] out, He took the father and the mother of the child, and those who were with Him, and entered where the child was lying.

(verses 37, 40b)

"So, how did the interview go on Friday, honey?" Betty asked Dwayne as he and Sherry settled in for a weekend visit.

"Pretty well, I think," Dwayne answered, munching a cookie. "The dean of the graduate school seems like a cool guy—for a dean. I mean, he seemed impressed with my grades and all. I think I have a good chance of getting in."

"Sherry, what did you think of the dean?" Betty asked while the two of them chopped the salad fixings.

"Well, he's got a nice office," Sherry laughed. "I waited outside while Dwayne talked to him."

"Oh," Betty said. Dwayne caught "something" in his mom's voice.

Later, while Sherry was upstairs, Betty sat down on the sofa next to Dwayne: "Honey, I want to tell you something your father did once that I don't think I've ever told you about. He had a big meeting with a client to discuss a contract that could have meant a lot of income. It was Will, his partner, Ron, and the men from the other company. He asked me to come to the meeting with him. He didn't explain my presence, only that I was his wife. I think he was saying to them, 'This is my wife and that's the reason she's here.' And he was saying to me, 'What *I* do, *we* do.' It turned out to be quite a romantic day."

"The meeting with the dean, right?" Dwayne grinned. "You don't miss much, do you, Mom?"

"Just an idea to tuck away, that's all, Dwayne. Not something you do every time, but at the right times."

From the Word

Romance in marriage is created by an unpredictable blend of timing, choices, and responses. It is more a dance than a march, with steps rarely repeated the same way twice. Though Jesus was not romancing the disciples, he used opportune moments to say to them, "You are My friends, My associates in a grand mission, and I want you to be with Me at this important time in My life."

Think how it must have made Peter, James, and John feel when Jesus took them with Him into a place where He worked a mighty miracle—after sending everyone else out! Do you think they felt privileged? More a part of Jesus' "team"? Undoubtedly! Whether in ministry or marriage, being included is a good feeling.

For the Heart

What is "important" in the lives of married couples will vary from marriage to marriage. But you know those areas which you tend to do by yourself—business, recreation, or hobbies. Whatever those private areas are, can you consider opening them up on occasion to your spouse?

Be prepared: You might get turned down the first time or two you issue an invitation. But persevere! You'll be surprised where romance can be discovered! Your genuine desire to include your spouse in meaningful areas of your life will be received once the "shock" wears off!

"You want me? To go where? With you? Say, what are you up to?"

DEVOTIONAL 5

Security = Caring = Romance

SCRIPTURE
Deuteronomy 8:7–18

"... God is bringing you into a good land, a land of brooks of water, of fountains and springs, ... a land of wheat and barley, of vines and fig trees and pomegranates, a land of olive oil and honey."

(verses 7–8)

I had never experienced anything that felt so romantic, Lillith wrote in her journal. *And maybe "romantic" isn't even the right word. I don't know if I even know what romantic means. But it's the only word I know to use . . . Yes, romantic is the word. It was romantic. It's sad that I haven't felt it since. And I'm afraid I'll never feel it again.*

Pastor Burton had asked Lillith to spend some time over a period of weeks writing out her thoughts and feelings about her brief marriage to Larry. Though she resisted at first (it seemed too therapeutic, and she did NOT need therapy), she had actually begun to enjoy it more—and write more—as she got into it.

When I think of what was romantic about our engagement, wedding, and first few months of marriage, I think it was how complete everything seemed, she continued. *Both Larry and I had great jobs, had more money than we needed, and we spent it willingly on our relationship. We lacked for nothing in those days. All of our needs were met and our questions answered. It was secure—and secure for me is romantic.*

Why? Because it meant Larry cared. Our honeymoon was perfect. Our condo we bought was perfect. I could go on and on. And even though I managed a lot of the details, Larry was a more-than-willing provider. It made me feel cared for, secure, and romanced.

And where did romance go? Where do all good things go when you're not grateful for what you have? We woke up one day and it was gone.

From the Word

Provision. Looking ahead. Caring enough to go beyond the minimum to make someone's life have extra meaning. These are the things which give life, and relationships, a deep sense of rightness, a deep sense of security—and romance. They don't guarantee perfection, but they will put one a step ahead of disaster.

God cared for the nation of Israel in such a way. As His covenant partner, God wanted the best for Israel. In Deuteronomy 8:7–18, God describes the land He is providing for His "betrothed." It was to be a magnificent dwelling place, suitable in every way for a long and satisfying relationship.

For the Heart

What responsibilities do you have in your marriage which you could fulfill in such a way that says, "I love you and want to meet your needs in a way that is meaningful to you"?

You may prepare healthy meals, keep an attractive home and yard, provide sufficiently for financial needs, or plan for family recreational or spiritual time together. Whatever the area of responsibility, you will cultivate romance in your marriage by saying "I love you" with the quality of your practical provision for your spouse.

Quiz: Being cared for and secure is (*a*) Romantic (*b*) Very romantic.

SESSION 11

COMMUNICATION:
Speak the Truth in Love

*N*ot long after the wedding, couples often experience difficulty in communicating. Some retreat behind silence... some erupt in anger... and some fail to listen. Learn to prepare your heart for meaningful communication in marriage!

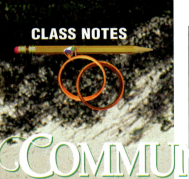

COMMUNICATION:
Speak the Truth in Love

INTRODUCTION

_____
_____
_____

n what ways is the tongue pictured in Scripture?

- Horse and _____ (James 3:2–3)
- Ship and _____ (James 3:4)
- _____ tongue (James 3:5a)
- Tongue as _____ (James 3:5b–6)
- Tongue as _____ (Proverbs 18:21)
- Tongue as _____ (Proverbs 12:18)

_____
_____

What fundamental principles of communication are presented in James 1:19?

1. Swift to _____

2. Slow to _____

3. Slow to _____

What is the proper response to anger?

A _____, gentle answer (Proverbs 15:1)

How does Ephesians 4:25–32 portray godly communication?

1. Don't _____.

2. Speak the _____.

3. Be angry and _____ _____.

4. _____ immediately.

What root problem must be addressed in order to have healthy communication?

_____ _____ your heart.

CONCLUSION

_____

_____

_____

EVALUATION

Communication: Speak the Truth in Love

Attitudes are at the very heart of either success or failure to communicate meaningfully in marriage. Take this evaluation to discern how well you are dealing with the challenge of communication in your marriage.

Remember, this assessment should be taken with an eye on the big picture of your marriage. Then, you'll be better prepared to discover what steps you can take toward healthy communication with your spouse.

Couples, are you enjoying healthy communication in your marriage? Total your score below.

		False		Sometimes			True
A	We are able to communicate clearly and don't experience any difficulty in understanding one another.	1	2	3	4	5	6	7
B	Neither of us retreats behind a wall of silence when we are frustrated or angry.	1	2	3	4	5	6	7
C	We both practice listening with interest, attentiveness, and good eye contact.	1	2	3	4	5	6	7
D	Neither of us demonstrates a pattern of vindictive, hurtful, or harsh speech.	1	2	3	4	5	6	7
E	We have learned to lower our voices and speak gently when emotions are running high.	1	2	3	4	5	6	7
F	We don't lie to each other, but always speak truthfully.	1	2	3	4	5	6	7
G	When we do disagree and have an argument, we seek to reconcile our differences before the day is over.	1	2	3	4	5	6	7
H	We are both courteous, kind, and gracious in how we speak to one another.	1	2	3	4	5	6	7

Column Subtotals:

The Couple's "Communication" Score
- **48–56** "Take all the time you need. I'm listening."
- **38–47** "Let me tell you what I think."
- **28–37** "Let's talk while we watch the game."
- **18–27** "Yeah, I'm listening . . . Wow, what a play!"
- **8–17** "What? Did you say something?"

GRAND TOTAL:

11.4   A BIBLICAL PORTRAIT OF MARRIAGE   © 1995 by Dr. Bruce H. Wilkinson and Walk Thru the Bible Ministries, Inc. Do not reprodu

1 Why are communication problems so infrequent during courtship yet so typical in most marriages?

2 What types of issues can create conflict in marriage? What are some of the underlying causes for any conflict?

3 How do people respond when someone listens to them attentively? What does it take to be a good listener?

4 How have you observed someone communicating anger nonverbally? How are acceptance and openness conveyed nonverbally?

5 What are the benefits of making up quickly after a disagreement? What are the consequences of delayed reconciliation?

PROJECT: PRACTICE COMMUNICATING

To learn how to slow down and minimize the potential for conflict, "**Think Five.**" **Post** the number "5" in various places throughout your home, car, and place of employment. Anytime you find yourself tempted to quickly react in anger or defensiveness, **mentally count to 5**—then respond in a soft, controlled fashion. When you are naturally inclined to criticize or speak negatively, count to 5. In a conversation, if you find yourself waiting for your spouse to pause so you can begin talking, take 5 and listen. **Practice** this technique for one week and see if you can be "swift to hear, slow to speak, and slow to wrath."

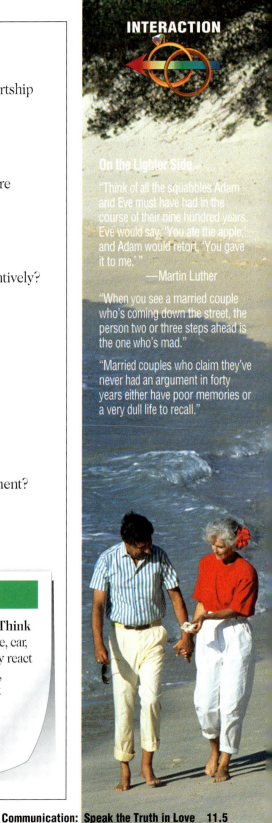

INTERACTION

On the Lighter Side...

"Think of all the squabbles Adam and Eve must have had in the course of their nine hundred years. Eve would say, 'You ate the apple,' and Adam would retort, 'You gave it to me.'"
—Martin Luther

"When you see a married couple who's coming down the street, the person two or three steps ahead is the one who's mad."

"Married couples who claim they've never had an argument in forty years either have poor memories or a very dull life to recall."

BIBLE STUDY

COMMUNICATION

The Tongue: Weapon or First Aid?

It is easy to be slow to hear, swift to speak, and swift to wrath—the direct opposite of God's design. All too often you may find yourself living with regret over something you have said that hurt someone else deeply. Or you may have been a victim of someone else's harsh and damaging comments.

In these studies, discover firsthand God's plan for communication that brings healing. Consider how you can personally bring life to your mate by how you speak, listen, accept, and forgive.

1. Listen Quickly — James 1:19–20

In what specific area is a person to be "swift"?

What hinders some people from being good listeners?

In your marriage, how can you tell when your spouse is listening to you?

For what specific topic of conversation does your spouse most desire your undivided attention?

2. Speak Wisely — Proverbs 10:19

How does this verse describe the person who restrains his lips?

What does it mean for someone to "restrain" his lips?

In what areas of your marriage are you inclined to say too much?

Describe a recent situation in your marriage when you acted wisely and held back from saying too much.

What mental and/or spiritual steps would help you learn to be wise in your speech?

11.6 A BIBLICAL PORTRAIT OF MARRIAGE

© 1995 by Dr. Bruce H. Wilkinson and Walk Thru the Bible Ministries, Inc. Do not reproduce.

3. Diffuse Anger
Proverbs 15:1

What kind of answer suppresses anger?

What does the word "soft" mean besides low in volume?

What emotions do you experience when your spouse speaks harshly to you?

What subjects tend to provide the greatest temptation for you to speak harshly to your mate?

In what particular subject would your soft answer most encourage your spouse?

4. Reconcile Promptly
Ephesians 4:26–27

In what time frame does this passage indicate conflicts are to be resolved?

Why is it so important to settle disputes quickly?

Describe a time in your marriage when an argument lasted for several days.

In what other areas of your marriage did you find it difficult to respond positively toward your spouse during that time?

What hinders you and your spouse from clearing up arguments quickly?

What one thing will you do differently the next time you have a disagreement with your spouse?

5. Speak Lovingly
Ephesians 4:15

How is a person to speak the truth?

Why is it often hard to hear the truth?

Describe a time in your marriage when your spouse truthfully and lovingly told you how he or she felt.

Is there anything you would like to honestly and openly share with your mate? How could you say it in love?

Will you submit yourself to God's guidelines for healthy communication? Signify your commitment to be quick to hear, slow to speak, and slow to wrath by initialing and dating this page.

_____
Your initials and date

Communication: Speak the Truth in Love   11.7

DEVOTIONAL 1

Sometimes Slower Is Better

SCRIPTURE: James 1:19–20

Therefore, my beloved brethren, let every man be swift to hear, slow to speak, slow to wrath; for the wrath of man does not produce the righteousness of God.

Bob Ethridge, Sr.,—"Mr. Take-Care-of-What-You-Own"—returning from an errand, jammed the brake pedal to the floor. He sat staring at the smashed-in passenger's side of Alice's car. Alice's just-paid-for car.

His mental ticker tape began flowing like an old-fashioned news wire: *WhathasAlicedone now!Howmanytimes haveIwarnedherabout foolingwiththetapeplayer whileshe'sdriving?Man theinsuranceratesare goingtogothroughtheroof! IwonderifAliceisokay? ForgivemeLordforthinking aboutthecarfirst.Butman whatwasAlicedoingtolet thishappen?...*

And on it went. Bob's anger was quickly getting the best of him as he sat fuming, staring at Alice's car. So absorbed was he that it took a beep of a car horn to jar him back to reality. Looking in the rearview mirror he saw Alice and a friend behind him in Alice's car—*ALICE'S CAR?! What in the world? ... How could Alice be in her ... Whose car is that in ...*

Not knowing whether to laugh or cry, Bob pulled to the curb and started to get out when it hit him: "Swift to hear, slow to speak, slow to wrath." He sat for a second, agreeing with God.

"Alice, I thought ... uh, whose car is ... Are you okay? ... Hi, Marge ..."

"Oh," Alice laughed. "You thought the damaged car was mine! No, honey. Don't you remember when Lew and Marge bought the exact same car we did from the rental company?"

"O-h-h-h, yes. Now I do. Right, right. So, uh, how's everything?"

📖 From the Word

Bob was on the verge of jumping to all sorts of conclusions. Correction: He *had* jumped to all sorts of conclusions. Thankfully, Alice in the mirror and a verse in his memory restrained him.

The Apostle James knew the tendency of the human heart to leap before looking. He wrote to the early church a life-and-relationship-saving piece of advice on how to communicate: "Listen first, speak only after listening, and save your anger for those few-and-far-between instances where the righteousness of God can genuinely be demonstrated by righteous indignation" (see James 1:19–20). Communicate calm—and calmly—when you speak!

♥ For the Heart

Is there any cauldron of communication that boils more dangerously than marriage? Probably not. More mountains in your marriage began as reactions to molehills than you would care to believe, most likely.

Would you purpose today—right now, before the Lord—that you will take James' words to heart, and then "to tongue"? There is a good chance that within 48 hours from now, you will have an opportunity to speak first, listen last (if at all), and get good and mad at your spouse. But you do not have to, if you'll agree with God.

Listening quickly and speaking slowly leaves no time for anger.

11.8   A BIBLICAL PORTRAIT OF MARRIAGE   © 1995 by Dr. Bruce H. Wilkinson and Walk Thru the Bible Ministries, Inc. Do not reproduce.

DEVOTIONAL 2

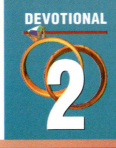

What Does Anger Feed On?

SCRIPTURE: Proverbs 15:1

A soft answer turns away wrath, but a harsh word stirs up anger.

Coming in the back door, Bob thought he heard his name mentioned. Setting the groceries on the counter, he went to investigate.

Deb was in the den, ironing shirts, and talking to her mom on the speaker phone. Or rather, *listening* to her mom on the speaker phone.

Seeing Bob, Deb put her finger to her lips. Realizing he was one of the topics of "conversation," he decided to listen in.

"Now, Deb," her mother continued, "you all have two children to put through college in a few years and I don't see how you plan to do it on Bob's salary alone. I get so frustrated with you both! I'm afraid you're going to be coming to your father and me to help you out when you should be working yourself, or Bob should be looking for a better job, to earn more money. Are you listening to me?" Deb's mother's tone was moving past advice, past frustration, and into the angry zone.

"Yes, I'm here, Mom. And I want you to know how glad I am to have parents that really care about me, and about their grandchildren. That means a lot, Mom," Deb replied softly. Bob was impressed.

He shook his head and tiptoed out of the room to go about his Saturday chores. Later, he asked Deb how the conversation ended.

"Oh, fine. I just put up a big soft feather pillow to deflect her frustration. I think she got a little embarrassed at being so angry when she saw I wasn't. The storm blew over pretty quickly! It takes two to tangle, you know, Bob."

From the Word

Deb was practicing a common-sense approach to communication which some have discovered by chance, but which many others have discovered from Scripture in Proverbs 15:1. The quickest way to keep any communication process from escalating into a full-scale war is for one of the parties to turn anger away with soft answers. It is definitely true that angry words feed off other angry words. But, as in nature, if the food supply is removed, the species soon dies out. Nothing stirs up and inflames anger like other angry people saying more angry things. And nothing puts out the fire of anger like a gentle and soaking shower of soft responses. Try it and you'll see!

For the Heart

In your marriage, or perhaps with your in-laws, you can probably identify a "hot topic" that is like an open container of gas—it just takes a spark to set it off. Surface the subject, and suddenly you're in a firestorm you didn't ask for. You not only didn't ask for the argument, you likewise are not required to participate in it.

Will you identify that "hot topic" right now and agree, by faith, to attempt to turn the other person's anger away the next time that topic, or any other hot topic, comes up?

Take God at His Word and move into anger-free communication!

Speak softly and make anger an endangered species in your world.

DEVOTIONAL 3

Do I Really Need to Know?

SCRIPTURE: Proverbs 26:20

Where there is no wood, the fire goes out; and where there is no talebearer, strife ceases.

"Who in the world?..." Betty wondered on a Thursday night when her doorbell rang three times in a row. Before she could lay her sewing down and get to the door, Lillith opened the door and barged in.

"Lillith! Oh, I'm glad it's you. You scared me!" Betty said, relaxing into a grin. "What's got my little sister so energized on an otherwise calm night?"

"Don't start the 'little sister' bit, Betty. I'm in no mood. I am so mad I could... well, whatever! I'm just furious! I didn't know where else to go so I came here."

"Well, come in—and sit down. What in the world happened?"

"The usual—it's Larry again. Isn't it always? I just ran into him at the mall and got so mad talking to him I had to leave! I'm sure Mother has told you what he's been doing lately—I told her all this a week ago," Lillith fumed.

"No," Betty looked puzzled, "Mom hasn't mentioned Larry. I talked to her just last night for a long time, and we discussed lots of family things, you know, just newsy stuff, and she didn't mention Larry at all."

"Well, you need to know this. First of all, he's always saying that he can't afford to increase Allison's child support when I know good and well..."

Betty held up her hand like a policeman in a Manhattan intersection:

"Lillith, wait. I think maybe there's a reason Mother didn't mention this to me. I have no reason to think badly of Larry, even if you do. It helps to talk things out sometimes, but I'd rather not hear things I don't need to know, okay?"

From the Word

Betty is about to do something thoroughly Biblical and almost unheard-of in modern communication venues, whether secular or Christian. She is about to dam up a rushing torrent of unneeded and inappropriate information before it drowns her own soul. She is about to excuse herself from being used as fuel to feed an out-of-control blaze that could potentially consume Lillith and her in a matter of moments. She is doing what the writer of Proverbs 26:20 says to do: Don't become a talebearer or encourage a talebearer by listening to their words. Is it sometimes necessary to hear negative information about another person? It may be, but in the majority of cases, it is not. So don't!

For the Heart

One of the greatest dangers to your marriage, and the long-term well-being of your relationship, comes from relating private information about your spouse to a friend or outsider.

Is the information correct? It could be, but it is usually presented in an emotional, biased context. Can the outsider fix, or correct, the fault of the spouse? Hardly ever. Does the outsider go away with a more positive view of the one being discussed? No.

If you have participated in talebearing about your spouse, please go quickly and apologize to the one to whom you spoke. Put out the fire today.

Gossip is an all-consuming thing, devouring subject and messenger.

DEVOTIONAL 4

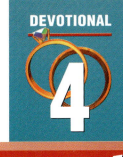

To Tell the Truth

SCRIPTURE: Matthew 5:33–37

"But let your 'Yes' be 'Yes,' and your 'No,' 'No.' For whatever is more than these is from the evil one." (verse 37)

Dwayne and Sherry were meeting for lunch at the campus snack shop.

"Hi, Dwayne. You're coming from French class, aren't you? Let me guess: You got your project back, and it wasn't a C like you thought. Am I right or am I right?"

"Uh, right, Sherry. We got them back, and right again, it wasn't a C," Dwayne laughed nervously.

"I knew it. You're a genius! The world's next Nobel Prize winner, buying me a burger and fries. I can't believe it," Sherry clowned.

Later that night, when Sherry stopped by Dwayne's dorm lobby to study together, Dwayne's manner was clearly subdued.

"Sweetie, you okay?" Sherry asked. "Why the long face?"

Dwayne looked down while Sherry waited for an answer. "Sherry, I wasn't totally honest with you at lunch about my French project. You asked if it was a C like I feared it might be, and I said, 'No'—and it wasn't. But the real truth is, it was worse. I made a D."

"O·h·h," Sherry said softly.

"I'm sorry I kind of fibbed about it to you. I guess my pride got in the way."

After a few silent moments, Sherry confronted Dwayne: "Dwayne, I love you, come A, B, C, D, or F. You know that. But the grade isn't my concern. If you and I are going to be married, we've got to have an understanding: Yes means yes, and no means no. Period. No dancing around. No games. No half-truths. You knew what I was asking, didn't you? If we can't trust each other's words, Dwayne, what kind of marriage will we have?"

From the Word

Sherry is not the only person for whom the meaning of yes and no is a serious issue. Take Jesus Christ, for example. He lived in a day in which duplicity among leaders was common. The Pharisees would often say one thing, but mean another, and rationalize the difference.

Christ brought a totally new perspective to communication. His words on the subject are recorded in Matthew 5:33-37. The essence of His teaching is this: If the answer is yes, say, "Yes." If the answer is no, say, "No." Don't say, "I swear," or "I promise." This raises people's suspicions so they may think, "Are you trying to convince me of something?" The essence of trustworthiness in communication is simplicity.

For the Heart

In your marriage, how do you and your spouse measure up on the "trustworthiness-in-communication" scale? When your spouse tells you something, do you give it a second or third thought, wondering if it is totally true or accurate? How does your spouse treat your words?

If either of you has ever been less than honest with the other, it can take time to rebuild a shattered communication environment. If there is a need, express clearly to your spouse your intent to tell "the truth, the whole truth, and nothing but the truth."

Telling the truth means not having to recall what you said.

DEVOTIONAL 5

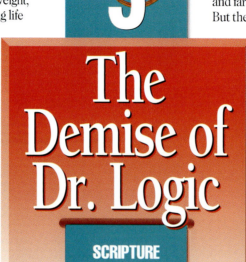

The Demise of Dr. Logic

SCRIPTURE: Ephesians 4:29

Let no corrupt communication proceed out of your mouth, but what is good for necessary edification, that it may impart grace to the hearers.

"Well, Deb, I'm thinking that the best way to solve this would be for you to grow up and get over this preoccupation with your weight. I mean, if you want to lose the weight, lose it. If you don't, quit making life miserable for everyone by whining about it so much!"

"G-r-o-w u-p?!" Deb responded. "Who's advising whom to 'grow up'? You're the one who whined for two weeks about having to miss the company fishing tournament because of a family commitment. And you're also the same 'Mr. Maturity' who couldn't control his greed and bought new tools we couldn't afford. Right? You've got some nerve telling me to grow up!"

"Okay, how about if I not *tell* you, but I *ask* you to grow up? Does that satisfy you?" Bob retorted.

"Ohhhhh, men! You think everything is so simple for everyone else. If you lived up to just half of what you expect me to live up to, you'd be a walking, talking example of perfection!"

"So now my sin is that I'm a man, is it? Deb, you need to learn to argue in addition to losing weight. First, you attack *me,* then *all* men, because you can't defend your premise," Bob countered, confident in his logic.

"Well, you can finish this argument by yourself, 'Dr. Logic.' I don't have to put up with this," Deb said as she ran sobbing from the room.

Bob sat on the bed, staring at the floor. His wife was downstairs weeping. Bobby and Kim were standing in the doorway, looking worried. And he was trying to figure out where the words he just uttered could have come from.

From the Word

A sad night in the Ethridge home. Fortunately for Bob and Deb, these kinds of nights had been few and far between in their marriage. But they do happen, even in the best of marriages, and to the most loving of couples.

This kind of talk, everyone knows, accomplishes nothing. It is, in the words of the Apostle Paul, "corrupt communication." What is corrupt communication? It is the transmission of a message that is ineffective for any number of reasons. Perhaps the content itself is either untrue or unwise. Perhaps the transmission system itself breaks down. Regardless, Paul says to avoid it. It neither edifies nor encourages.

For the Heart

When you summarize all that the Bible says on the subject, it boils down to this: Help people, not hurt them, with your communication.

How about in your marriage? Is unwholesome or derogatory language common? If yes, it is only common because Scripture is not being obeyed. If you do not stop it now, it will only become worse. Language is habitual. How you talk now is how you will talk in the future—only to a greater degree.

Pray and ask God to give you speech that builds up, not that tears down. It's what the Bible says to do.

Your words build the dwelling in which your marriage lives.

LOYALTY:
Love with *All* Your Heart

SESSION 12

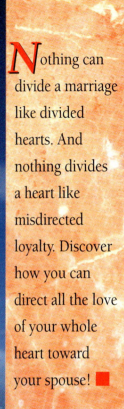

Nothing can divide a marriage like divided hearts. And nothing divides a heart like misdirected loyalty. Discover how you can direct all the love of your whole heart toward your spouse!

CLASS NOTES

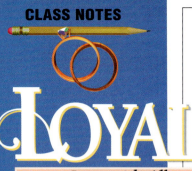

LOYALTY
Love with *All* Your Heart

INTRODUCTION

_____

_____

_____

What is the real source of true loyalty in marriage?

Loyalty is an issue of the _____.

_____

_____

Through what types of activities can a husband's or wife's loyalty be eroded?

- _____ friendships with the _____ sex
- Soaps = _____ _____
- Romance _____
- _____ magazines
- _____ _____ videos

W LOYALTY

What are God's commands regarding adultery (Exodus 20:14, 17; Matthew 5:27–28, 31–32; Matthew 19:4–6)?

H LOYALTY

How does God respond to adultery (1 Thessalonians 4:4–8; Hebrews 13:4)?

CONCLUSION

EVALUATION

**Loyalty:
Love with *All*
Your Heart**

Though sometimes painfully evident, a lack of loyalty is usually hidden from view for quite some time. Loyalty really is an issue of the heart.

Take this quiz from your individual point of view only—not as a couple. Simply examine yourself in light of the truths taught in this session.

Evaluate yourself to determine the depth of your loyalty to your spouse. Total your score below.

		False		Sometimes			True
A	I demonstrate my emotional loyalty by alerting my spouse to people or situations that are pulling at my affections.	1	2	3	4	5	6	7
B	I avoid situations that might provide the opportunity for me to become attracted to someone of the opposite sex.	1	2	3	4	5	6	7
C	I guard my heart from the influence of sexually suggestive television programs, videos, or reading material.	1	2	3	4	5	6	7
D	I do not look at pornography or sexually graphic materials.	1	2	3	4	5	6	7
E	I do not give in to the temptation to entertain lustful thoughts about others in my imagination.	1	2	3	4	5	6	7
F	I am physically faithful to my spouse and do not engage in adulterous relationships.	1	2	3	4	5	6	7
G	I employ safeguards in my life to help me be accountable when facing sexual temptation.	1	2	3	4	5	6	7
H	I am committed to guard my heart and mind at all costs.	1	2	3	4	5	6	7

Column Subtotals:

Your "Loyalty" Score
- **48–56** Well done, good and faithful spouse!
- **38–47** Keep working at it . . . you're almost there.
- **28–37** You can strengthen the weak areas.
- **18–27** There's no better place or time to start.
- **8–17** God forgives—and He can restore.

GRAND TOTAL:

1 How is marital faithfulness (or the lack thereof) portrayed in the media today? What values drive this portrayal?

2 What are some of the ways someone could have an "affair" besides committing physical adultery with another person?

3 Why is it so difficult to confront a person who appears to be guilty of emotional adultery? How should a person be confronted who is guilty of physical adultery?

4 What are some of the ways that loyalty from the heart can be demonstrated?

5 In what ways might a church encourage its couples in their commitment to marital faithfulness?

PROJECT: BECOME A LOYAL SPOUSE

It is vital to guard your heart from being pulled to anyone or anything other than your spouse. **Decide** what boundaries you need to put in place concerning how you relate to the opposite sex: where and when to meet or dine, how to touch and hug, how to give compliments (and what or what not to compliment on), what to converse about, how to avoid flirting, and how to make eye contact. Also **develop** any needed safeguards in regard to your own heart: what you will (and won't) read or watch, to whom you will be accountable for your thoughts and actions, etc. **Verbalize** your boundaries with your spouse as an evidence of your loyalty.

INTERACTION

On the Lighter Side

"Knit your hearts with an unslipping knot."
—William Shakespeare

"A woman feels a man's love should be like a toothbrush. It shouldn't be shared."

"There are a lot more marital arguments over a wink than a mink."

"It takes two to make a marriage a success, and only one to make it a failure."

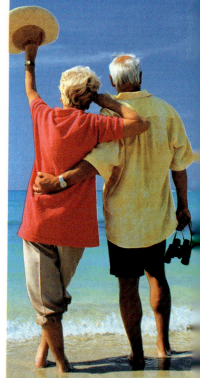

BIBLE STUDY

LOYALTY

Part or All of Your Heart?

Loyalty may be reflected in actions, but it really is a heart issue. Are you withholding any part of your heart from your spouse? Are you allowing other people and activities to become the center of your affections? Or are you unquestionably loyal to your spouse with all your heart?

As you read these Scriptures and answer the following questions, allow God to search your heart to see how much of your heart is loyal to your spouse.

1 Broken Loyalty
Matthew 19:5–6

What is man instructed not to do in relation to marriage?

What can a person do that tears apart a marriage?

What have you recently done that you know put some distance between you and your spouse?

What can you do to seek to counteract the negative results of such an action?

2 Guard Your Mind
Matthew 5:27–28

What does Jesus say constitutes adultery?

Why do you think Jesus widened the definition of adultery from what was stated in the Old Testament?

How much do you struggle with the temptation to commit mental adultery?

On a practical level, how do you most commonly succumb to mental adultery?

What do you need to do to guard against giving in to mental adultery?

12.6 A BIBLICAL PORTRAIT OF MARRIAGE

© 1995 by Dr. Bruce H. Wilkinson and Walk Thru the Bible Ministries, Inc. Do not reproduce

3. Guard Your Eyes
Psalm 101:3a

What guidelines did the psalmist use in relation to wicked things?

Why is it so important not to look at things that are ungodly?

At what types of "wicked" things are you inclined to look?

How is your heart drawn away from your mate when you set your eyes upon things that are evil or sensual?

In what specific ways do you need to guard your eyes?

4. An Open Heart
Proverbs 23:7c

In the last phrase of this verse, what comment is made about this man's heart?

Have you ever sensed that your spouse's heart wasn't with you?

What did your spouse do (or not do) that communicated a loss of loyalty?

How do you sometimes close your heart to your spouse?

What do you need to do to open your heart once again to your mate?

5. What God Sees
1 Samuel 16:7b

At what does the Lord look?

What does God see when he looks at *your* heart?

In looking at your heart, how would God describe your loyalty to your spouse?

What would the Lord most likely instruct you to correct so that you could love your mate with all your heart?

Will you guard your heart from all people, places, and activities that pull your loyalty away from your spouse? And will you make a fresh commitment to love your spouse with all your heart? Affirm your promise before God by initialing and dating this page.

Your initials and date

Loyalty: Love with All Your Heart

DEVOTIONAL 1

A Permanent Proposal

SCRIPTURE
Ecclesiastes 5:1–7

When you make a vow to God, do not delay to pay it; for He has no pleasure in fools. Pay what you have vowed. It is better not to vow than to vow and not pay.
(verses 4–5)

On New Year's Eve, the extended Ethridge family had gathered for a traditional time of reflection over the past year. The cider was spicy, the logs in the fireplace were simmering, and a light veil of silent snow had turned the house into a warm and cozy cocoon.

Bob and Alice, Bob and Deb and their two children, Bobby and Kim, Betty and her son, Dwayne, and his fiancée, Sherry, and Lillith and her daughter, Allison—all were gathered in the room.

"In light of Dwayne's and Sherry's engagement this year," Bob, Sr., began amidst murmurs of approval, "I had asked each of you to prepare something to share with them about marriage. And I'm going to ask Dwayne and Sherry to go first and tell us what they've learned this year during their engagement. Dwayne and Sherry, the floor is yours. And remember—no pressure!"

"Right!" Dwayne said, laughing along with the group. "Well, I'll start and Sherry, maybe you can finish.

"I guess the most challenging thought for me is what a serious commitment marriage is. One of Sherry's pastors gave us a verse about keeping your vows before God—'don't vow if you're not going to pay'—and that really hit me hard. I've seen all of you try to do that—and Aunt Lillith, I know this has been a rough year for you, but I've learned some good things from your situation, too, which I appreciate. So I'm just thankful to have been warned ahead of time—'This is the big one. Make sure!' And, thankfully, I am sure—*very* sure."

From the Word

Wise words from a young man just getting his bearings on the lifelong journey of marriage. The verse Dwayne and Sherry had been given in their premarital counseling is Ecclesiastes 5:5, "It is better not to vow than to vow and not pay." These words are taken from the ancient Near Eastern practice of covenant-making. And marriage is, Scripturally speaking, a lifelong covenant between two people—a covenant with permanent implications. To break a covenant for casual reasons—even for what could be called "good" reasons—was a source of shame to both parties. A marriage covenant not kept would have been better not made at all.

For the Heart

In most modern cultures in the world, the marriage covenant is treated lightly. Divorce is prominent, if not rampant. And it has touched many Christians.

Whether you have been through a divorce, or have entertained the thought of divorcing, or are in a stable marriage where divorce does not seem likely, would you do the following? At the beginning of this week of devotionals on "Loyalty" in marriage, bow in prayer and renew your vow to God that the marriage you are living in is the marriage you will die in, as far as it is up to you.

Again: It is better not to vow, than to vow and not pay.

DEVOTIONAL 2

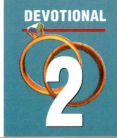

The Pit Bull of Love

SCRIPTURE
Song of Solomon 8:6–7

Many waters cannot quench love, nor can the floods drown it. If a man would give for love all the wealth of his house, it would be utterly despised.

(verse 7)

"Mr. Chairman," Bob, Jr., began, addressing his dad in a put-on voice, "may the record reflect that these *profound* comments on marriage were delivered by none other than *my nephew*."

"Duly noted, Son," Bob, Sr., panned dryly. "Since you've been so moved, why don't you and Deb go next. What can you two share with Dwayne and Sherry?"

"Well, as much as I hate to admit it, there were some rough spots for us in our marriage this year. Actually," Bob clarified, "some rough spots for *me* that made it rough for Deb. There was a time where, for a few weeks, I sort of gave up. I just got tired of all the pressures of work, and marriage, and family. I think I made an unconscious decision to just coast, to basically stop trying—and caring."

While Bob's feelings were catching up with his words, Deb joined in: "I sort of just realized one day how Bob was feeling. And I wasn't sure what to do. I was a little scared, frankly."

"But," Bob continued, taking Deb's hand, "what you *did* do saved me, and us. Deb wouldn't give up on our love, even though she was the only one doing much loving at the time. She refused to let me believe that I didn't care. She was like a pit bull on a robber's ankle—she just wouldn't let go! She took some money she had saved for new furniture and surprised me with a weekend at a lodge so we could get away and talk things through. And—here we are tonight, thanks to Deb's loyalty, and her not letting my discouragement quench our love."

From the Word

What Bob went through is not unusual, is it? Every married person goes through periods occasionally of discouragement—even despair. What is a bit more unusual is how Deb responded. Often, if one spouse grows discouraged, the other gets fearful or insecure, and begins pulling back as well. Thankfully, Deb did the opposite. She lived out what Song of Solomon 8:6–7 describes: *Many waters cannot quench the fire of love, nor can floods drown it. Love and its preservation are even more valuable than money for those who realize it.* Nothing is more valuable than love, and nothing is more worth fighting for when it appears to be slipping away. The fire of true love is unquenchable.

For the Heart

Have there been times in your marriage when you or your spouse have fallen prey to discouragement over the trials of love? Perhaps even now one of you is in that condition.

Whether it is today, or at a time in the future, you or your spouse will need each other to fight for your love. Can you do that? Can you be the strong and loyal partner if it is your spouse who is weak? Yes, you can! If you will decide today that it is your marital duty to push back the waters that would drown your love. Strengthen your loyalty today—feed the fire of your love—and be prepared!

Only a few things in life are worth fighting for. Love is one of them.

Loyalty: Love with All Your Heart

DEVOTIONAL 3

Loyal and Devoted by Choice

**SCRIPTURE
1 Corinthians 7:8**

But I say to the unmarried and to the widows: It is good for them if they remain even as I am.

"Thanks, Bob—and thank you, Deb. We don't always know the dramas that the Lord is working out in each of our lives, do we?" Bob, Sr., reflected quietly.

"Dwayne and Sherry," Bob, Sr., winked, re-energizing the group, "I hope you two are taking notes on all this free advice you're getting. This is good stuff! Okay—next?"

"Well, since I'm the mom and the 'mom-in-law' of the honored couple, maybe I should share a few thoughts," Betty spoke up.

"This will be different, I guess, since I'm obviously no longer married," she continued. "But when Dwayne and Bob both touched on how loyalty, or lifelong devotion in marriage, was what they had learned about, that struck a chord with me.

"Since Will died, I've been content to live as a widow and not remarry. It seems that Scripture encourages widows to take that option if they can. And while I don't understand all the reasons for it, I've learned that for me, loyalty to what God says in His Word about marriage is always the best policy.

"I don't have a husband to be loyal and devoted to, but I do have a heavenly Father. And I know that if Will could send me a message from heaven, he would probably say, 'Look to God in His Word. It is there that you will find whatever direction you need concerning any aspect of marriage.'"

"Dwayne and Sherry, if you will show your loyalty and devotion to each other by first being loyal and devoted to God and His Word, your marriage will be a lifelong success!"

From the Word

Good advice from one who has practiced what she is preaching. Often the principles of God's Word are not the easiest of all possible choices. But they always produce the highest character and build the greatest faith.

Why did Paul recommend that widows remain single—to which Betty had sought to be loyal (1 Corinthians 7:8)? In 1 Corinthians, the practical side of life is considered. And practically speaking, a widow, watched over and cared for by the church and her extended family, can devote the rest of her days to serving the Lord and advancing His kingdom. The easiest choice? Maybe not. But it is a Biblical one.

For the Heart

No Christian spouse can be loyal and devoted to a husband or wife who is not first loyal and devoted to God and His Word. There is no room for compromise!

How are you demonstrating loyalty to your spouse? What principles have you learned in this seminar which you have taken to heart and want to practice? List them now—turn back through this workbook to refresh your memory. Make a fresh commitment to God that He, His Word, and His chosen spouse for you will receive your loyalty from this day forth!

Heart status, not marital status, is most important to God.

DEVOTIONAL 4

Everyone Learns Something

SCRIPTURE: Luke 14:25–35

After Betty's words, the crackling of the logs on the hearth was the only sound. Sherry broke the silence, saying what everyone was thinking: "Wow, Betty. I've never known anyone who wasn't married who knew so much about marriage. I mean, it makes me think that I could be learning a lot about marriage just by studying the Bible more."

"That's a good word, Sherry," Bob, Jr., added. "And I think I know someone else who, though not married, has learned a lot about marriage this past year. Sis, have we been saving the best for last?"

"I don't know, Bob," Lillith answered, a bit embarrassed. "I don't think I have much I can share with Dwayne and Sherry about marriage. I think I've mostly learned what *not* to do."

"Hey, Aunt Lillith, we'll take it all! Right, Sherry?" Dwayne volunteered.

"You bet! Lillith, I'd really love to know your thoughts on marriage. You've been through a whole different set of circumstances than anyone else. Please share with us," Sherry added, feeling bad for Lillith's predicament, and wanting to make her feel needed.

"Thanks, Sherry," Lillith said, putting a finger to the corner of her eye, but failing to contain a tear. "I guess to summarize it all, I would say, 'count the cost' before you do anything—especially before getting married! I thought I had, but I found I was more proud and immature than I was loyal to my marriage. I had not counted the cost! I can only hope that I've learned something in the process."

> "For which of you, intending to build a tower, does not sit down first and count the cost . . . lest, after he has laid the foundation, and is not able to finish it, all who see it begin to mock him, saying, 'This man began to build and was not able to finish.'"
> (verses 28–30)

From the Word

Lillith is right on track. The principle she learned in her marriage to Larry is one that Christ Himself taught concerning the whole spiritual life. It is a life of discipline, of cost, and of sacrifice. And no one who is not prepared for the cost will succeed in building a deeper life—or a marriage.

When Christ spoke, as recorded in Luke 14:25–35, He spoke words which divide. They divide those who are serious about the kingdom of God from those who follow Christ to get something for free. And the same is true in marriage. The exhortation to count the cost can accomplish the same purpose: It can divide those who would marry for self-centered ends from those who marry to love and serve a spouse.

For the Heart

The longer you have been married, the more realistic you have had to become about why you married. Was it for something your spouse had that you wanted for yourself? Or, hopefully, was it for something you knew you could give to the life of the one you were marrying? Marriage is too costly, and the stakes too high, to marry for any other reason.

Perhaps you could share with your spouse how you believe your reasons for marrying him or her have matured over time. And how you are more convinced than ever that your decision was the right one!

Better to count costs beforehand than to pick up the pieces later.

Loyalty: Love with All Your Heart

DEVOTIONAL 5

Marriages Built on Prayer

"We're all still learning to be loyal, Lillith," Bob, Sr., said. "No one that I know is doing it perfectly, so you have plenty of company. Thanks for being so honest."

"Yeah, thanks, Aunt Lillith," Dwayne agreed. "Thanks for being so open with us."

"Well, I guess that leaves you and me, honey," Bob, Sr., said, turning to Alice. To the rest of the group, Bob continued: "Alice and I had already decided that the thing we would share would be about the importance of prayer in your marriage, Dwayne and Sherry. And, we agreed, that instead of talking about prayer, it would be better to pray! So, I'm going to ask us all to gather around Dwayne and Sherry here and I'll lead us in a prayer for their new marriage."

The group gathered around the young couple, standing silently for a moment before the patriarch spoke:

"Gracious heavenly Father, thank You for each family represented here. Thank You for our whole, extended family, and for the love we share.

"We pray now for Dwayne and Sherry. Grant them a lifelong union, Lord. Grant them a fruitful and abundant relationship. Grant them a strong place of service in Your kingdom.

"Help Dwayne to lead and love. Grant that Sherry may help and submit. May they leave joyfully, and cleave to each other willingly. And may You remind them always to love each other as Christ has loved and forgiven them. I ask these things in Christ's name. Amen."

And all the family said, "Amen."

SCRIPTURE
Philippians 4:6–7

Be anxious for nothing, but in everything by prayer and supplication, with thanksgiving, let your requests be made known to God; and the peace of God, which surpasses all understanding, will guard your hearts and minds through Christ Jesus.

From the Word

Bob, Sr., certainly proved that wisdom comes with age, didn't he? From his own marriage of many years, and watching the marriages of his children, he learned that prayer is the foundation upon which everything is built.

Surely the Apostle Paul would agree. He said in Philippians 4:6–7 to let all—*all*—your requests be made known to God—and to do so without anxiety! Does marriage produce anxiety? At times it does. Are there problems that seem insurmountable? There can be. Could spouses ever use a healthy dose of the peace of God? Very definitely! And the way to be released from anxiety, find answers to problems, and receive God's peace—is by prayer.

For the Heart

Congratulations! You've completed the sixty daily devotionals for *A Biblical Portrait of Marriage*. You've considered the roles and responsibilities of the couple, the wife, and the husband. And you've studied some of the most challenging problem areas in marriage. Now that you're all dressed up, where do you go from here?

Why not go to the Lord in prayer, just as Bob Ethridge, Sr., did, and ask Him to bless to your understanding, and to your practice, all that you have learned in this course. Even better, take time to pray with your spouse. Then—begin looking for His answers!

Prayer: Where husbands and wives meet heart-to-heart.

WALK THRU THE BIBLE
Changing Lives All Over the World

Walk Thru the Bible's global ministry partners with the local church by providing relationships and resources to influential disciple makers throughout the world. From the Amazon River to the plains of Kenya, Walk Thru the Bible is changing lives and creating disciples for Christ on a daily basis.

- Over **13.5 million people** impacted by live teaching in the past five years
- Over **60 thousand pastors and teachers** trained in the past five years
- On-the-ground presence in over **60 countries**
- Strategic **network of local leaders** worldwide
- Intentional **interdenominational** impact

Global Ministry

Partnering for lasting life change through transferable, biblical teaching, training, and tools

To be a part of this movement, visit **www.walkthru.org** and click on donate.

Brand New
20th Anniversary
Daily Walk Bible

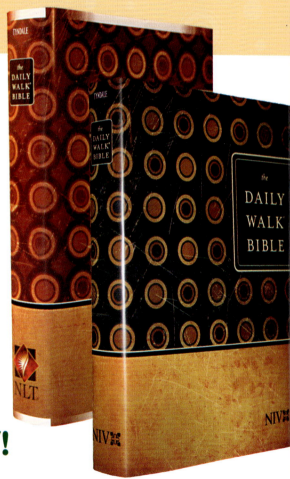

20% off
while supplies last

Great for gifts!

Great for small groups!

ORDER NOW!
www.walkthru.org

Free small-group resources online.

www.walkthru.org

Brand new DVD Series from Walk Thru the Bible available now at

raiseupachild.org

raise up a child

A BIBLICAL PORTRAIT OF PARENTING

Try it or buy it at **raiseupachild.org** or **walkthru.org**

800.361.6131

A PRODUCT OF

4201 NORTH PEACHTREE ROAD
ATLANTA, GEORGIA 30341
WWW.WALKTHRU.ORG
ORDERS: 800.361.6131

Know the Lover of your soul.

What do you want? Are you looking for an abundant life, real intimacy, and eternal purpose? Deep in your heart you crave these things, and deep in your heart is where God wants to meet you. Our devotional magazines will help you connect with Him and cultivate the only relationship that can give you lasting fulfillment. To find out more visit us at
www.devotionals.org.

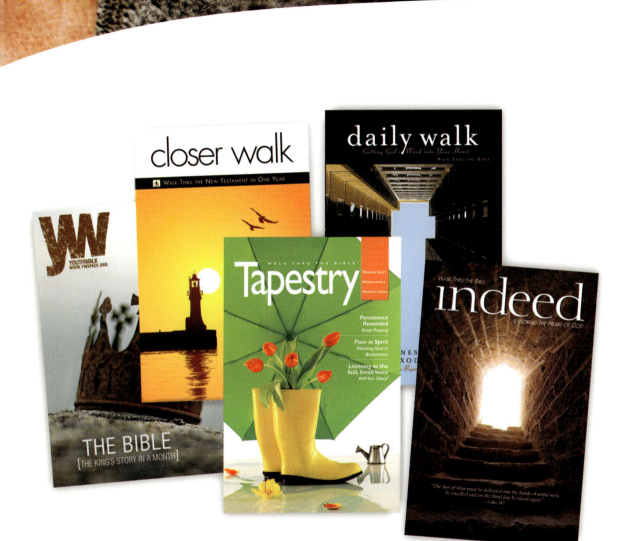

devotional**s**.org

A RESOURCE OF
WALK THRU THE BIBLE
4201 NORTH PEACHTREE ROAD
ATLANTA, GEORGIA 30341
www.walkthru.org
ORDERS 800.361.6131
PH 770.458.9300

NOTES

NOTES

NOTES

NOTES

NOTES